Spirit on the Water

Spirit on the Water

XI EXTRAORDINARY CRICKET TOURS

Mike Harfield

First Published March 2011

Published by Loose Chippings Books
The Paddocks
Chipping Campden
Gloucestershire
GL55 6AU
www.loosechippings.org

Printed and bound in Great Britain by MPG Biddles Ltd. King's Lynn

Hardback ISBN 978-1-907991-01-1
Paperback ISBN 978-0-9554217-9-2
Ebook ISBN 978-1-907991-02-8

To Vivyan for her friendship
and
Sir Vivian for his inspiration

Acknowledgements

Thanks to John Harfield for designing the cover and to Viv Whittaker for the original idea of the cover. Thanks also to Viv for the 'constructive feedback' she gave while I was writing the book. Thanks to Jill for crossing some 't's and dotting some 'i's. I'm also very grateful to Crawford Scholes who read the draft more than once. He did his best to correct my grammar and punctuation, and gave good advice on certain points of style. Most important of all, he spotted one or two cricket inaccuracies that had unaccountably slipped in!

Grateful thanks also to John Wisden & Co for their kind permission to reprint extracts from Wisden Cricketers' Almanack.

The Tours

		Page
Foreword		9
1.	Ash Tree CC tour of Menorca, 2000	13
2.	Aborigine tour of England, 1868	23
3.	West Indies tour of England, 1984	42
4.	Australia tour of India, 2001	60
5.	England tour of South Africa, 1913/14	69
6.	Ash Tree CC tour of Nantwich, 2007	96
7.	New Zealand tour of Australia, 1980/81	109
8.	West Indies tour of Australia, 1960/61	125
9.	West Indies tour of England, 1963	144
10.	England tour of Australia, 1928/29	166
11.	Ash Tree CC tour of Ibiza, 2010	187

Foreword

Vikings. They knew a thing or two about touring. Not for them complaints about the length of time away from home. Not for them the need for a flotilla of WAGs, kids and nannies to make the trip more bearable at Christmas time..... All they needed was a quick bonding session over a hog roast, a moment to pack up the sponsored long boat (not forgetting the pre-tour stop at the blacksmith's for kit) and then set sail over the perishing seas. And woe betides if you returned without the trophy.

Still, embarking upon a cricket tour (whether or not the spoils are a des-res in Valhalla) is a life-affirming prospect. The heady mix of venturing in to the unknown with a group of guys and finding yourselves standard bearers for your club/village/county/country brings people together in a way that a Sunday 3rd XI fixture in April never can.

When it comes to the cricket, few things are harder in sport than winning on tour. Not only are conditions alien – heat, insects, harder pitches, different balls, dodgy umpires – there are other perils designed to put you off your A game. For a start, there's no significant other to drag you out of the pub. You find yourself sharing a room with a bloke whose snoring could launch a shotgun start. Most shocking of all, you find that your "dress sense" is not a hindrance to the local ladies. No wonder you're struggling to find your metronomic line and length! Add those distractions to the fact that the locals think that your team is a joke and the further blow that your best player isn't travelling for "personal reasons" and you can see how tricky it's going to be.

It is not, however, impossible. Taking the group decision to embrace the different culture, smile in the face of adversity and undertaking to have the general attitude of work hard, play hard and enjoy, will turn a rag-tag bunch of individuals into a close fighting unit. From there, anything is possible.

Put it this way, the Vikings certainly had plenty to overcome, and, rumour has it, they made quite a fist of it. And, were it not for their highly questionable record on sexual equality and personal property, they would surely have gone down as the best tourists of all time.

Spirit on the Water doesn't include a Viking Tour, but it invokes the spirit and comradeship of touring to a tee.

Mark Butcher
Surrey and England

1. Ash Tree CC tour of Menorca, 2000

They say that you never forget your first time. In my case it is certainly true. She was warm and welcoming. Menorca in May, my first overseas cricket tour.

The year was 2000 and it was a minor miracle that the tour had taken place at all. There had been much speculation that aeroplanes would fall from the sky and computers would grind to a halt on the stroke of midnight at the start of the new millennium. Some people stockpiled food and others formed queues at cash dispensers on New Year's Eve. Not for the first or last time, the *Daily Mail* predicted the end of the world, as we know it.

In the event, the 'millennium bug' of Y2K proved to be a bit of a damp squib. Admittedly, in Australia, bus ticket validation machines in two states failed to operate and in the United States, 150 slot machines at racetracks in Delaware stopped working. The world somehow managed to cope with these potential disasters. More importantly, the Ash Tree Cricket Club were able to tour Menorca.

The Ash Tree is a Taverners cricket club, quite literally as it is named after a tavern near Macclesfield called The Ash Tree. What is Taverners cricket and how is it different from normal club cricket? Well, for a start, in Taverners cricket you are encouraged to sledge but only your own side, as in: "Get a move on Paul, the bar's open." In Taverners cricket, the proposed start time is invariably a best estimate. Experienced captains will tell certain players a start time of at least an hour earlier than the real one. Although it is nice to win, it really is the taking part that counts the most.

While we were in Menorca, a Test match was taking place at Lords and there was the usual abject batting display. This time however, it wasn't England but their opponents who were struggling. After seeming to lose to everyone throughout the 1990s, England had finally managed to find a team they could beat .... Zimbabwe.

Although it didn't really seem like it at the time, in retrospect, England had quite an interesting team that season. As Nass gave his usual intense, inspirational pep talk, who would have guessed what stars of the future were sitting round him in the changing room. Four players destined to be *Sky* commentators: Atherton, Hussain, Knight (cricket) and Giddins (poker), two Strictly Come Dancing winners (Gough and Ramprakash), one *BBC* radio commentator who would like to do more work for *Sky* (Stewart) and a DIY expert (Caddick). A promising Lancashire all-rounder (Flintoff), a young leg spinner on début (Schofield) and a player England had borrowed from the opposition, made up the rest of the team.

Nasser Hussain invited Zimbabwe to bat first and they were soon skittled out for 83. Ed Giddins got 5 for 15, a Test high for him. Darren Gough and Andrew Caddick got the other wickets. Top score for Zimbabwe was Andy Flower, later to become England's coach. At the time he was Zimbabwe's captain, leading batsman and wicket-keeper. He probably washed the kit and made the teas too.

When it was England's turn to bat they scored a creditable 415. Stewart made an undefeated century and celebrated with a hundred press-ups. Graeme Hick also scored a century against his native country. He was on 99 for a nervous twenty two minutes and he must have been worried that Mike Atherton would try and persuade Hussain to declare.[1] Eventually he got his century and was evidently so relieved that he relaxed his concentration, and Heath Streak had him LBW next ball.

Zimbabwe did not do much better second time around. They were bowled out for 123 with Gough, Caddick and Giddins again sharing the wickets. Flintoff only bowled three overs in the match and scored one run with the bat. This was marginally better than poor Chris Schofield who, in his first match for England, didn't bowl at all and got a third ball duck. He did get a bowl in the second Test against Zimbabwe, which ended in a draw, but probably wished he hadn't (0 for 73 off 18 overs). Interestingly, *Wisden* recorded that the two young Lancastrians, Flintoff and Schofield, appeared to lack the nous required at the highest level.

The Ash Tree would have welcomed either or both of them on our trip to Menorca that year. Indeed, Andrew Flintoff owns a house less than a mile from our home ground, so we have high hopes of recruiting him. Although he's retired now and based in Dubai, he should be OK for the occasional game of limited overs cricket and the Ash Tree CC cricket is very limited. So it seems a natural fit. We only play on Sundays. Everyone has to bowl three overs, so Freddie shouldn't get too tired during his spell. When batting, once you get to 30 you have to retire and come back at the end if everyone is out. If the sun is shining and the players are thirsty, beer is brought out to the fielding side and two batsmen halfway through the innings. If the sun isn't shining then beer is usually brought out anyway. The Ash Tree teas are famous for both their quality and quantity. A couple of seasons ago, someone introduced wine as an optional extra and that seems to have

---

1 Atherton famously declared England's second innings against Australia at Sydney in 1995 when Graeme Hick was on 98 not out.

stayed on as a regular fixture. Then Mark, a belligerent batsman and fearless fielder with a certain style, raised the bar by providing port and cheese as well. I can't help but think that Freddie would fit in well.

Back in 2000, Andrew Flintoff was still a promising young all-rounder who, it was said, "lacked the nous required at the highest level" so, coupled with the fact that he was required at Lords, he wasn't really a candidate for our Menorca tour.

We only planned to play one match in Menorca but we needed two days to prepare and then two days to recover. It might seem a long way to go to only play one 30-over-a-side cricket match but you would be surprised how much these games can take out of you.

Our morning flight from Manchester to Mahon left on time and, as it took off, my Ash Tree team-mate sitting next to me, pulled out a hip flask full of whisky. I mention this simply to illustrate the fact that when you are on a cricket tour, things happen. I had never seen David drink whisky before and I haven't seen him do it since. Equally, I'm pretty sure he doesn't take out a flask of whisky mid-flight when he goes on holiday with his family.

Unfortunately for David, the air-hostess spotted his flask and told him off like a scolded schoolboy. To avoid confiscation, he promised to put it away and not get it out again till we had landed safely in Menorca. He also agreed to write out 100 times "I must not take a hip flask of whisky on to an aircraft even if I am on a cricket tour". Nowadays of course, he wouldn't be able to get the flask through the multitude of security operations that you have to navigate just to get on the aeroplane. Even breast milk can be confiscated unless of course it is being carried *au naturel*.

We arrived at Mahon without further mishap and took the short trip to the hotel. We had two days preparation and acclimatisation to look forward to. I'm sure when England go abroad they head straight for the hotel gym and then start organising a net. At the Ash Tree, we believe that nets are greatly overrated and that it's important not to peak too early. The prevailing philosophy of the club is that it's no good wasting all your good shots in a net. Also, the generally held view is that gyms are to be avoided at all costs because of the risk of pulled muscles.

So we concentrated on 'acclimatisation' and team bonding. These are positive characteristics of a cricket tour that England has possibly neglected since the days of Beefy, Lamby and Porky.[2] If you share a beer with a team-mate in the early hours of the morning then you are less likely to be upset if he lets the ball through his legs off your bowling the next day. Of course, you could argue that drinking beer in the early hours tends to increase your chances of letting the ball through your legs the next day, but be that as it may.

Feeling fully acclimatised we set out, in brilliant sunshine, for our game against the MCC (Menorca Cricket Club). There are quite a few differences between Macclesfield and Menorca in May. The most obvious one, that we couldn't help but notice, is that it wasn't raining. What's more, it was wonderfully warm. At home, you would be trying to remember if you put that second, or maybe third, sweater in your cricket bag. You would probably be glancing anxiously at the sky and hoping that the huge black cloud goes away. More than likely, those players not out on the field would be congregating in the changing room trying to keep out of the wind.

Menorca Cricket Club has a delightful setting. As you drive through typical, parched, Mediterranean habitat, you arrive at an oasis of green and what is instantly recognisable as a cricket

2 I'm not sure Mike Gatting was ever called this but it seems too good an opportunity to miss!

ground. It's not a converted football pitch. It's not a dust bowl. It's a proper cricket ground with a scoreboard, sight-screens, a pavilion and a bar. The club has its own well, so is able to water the outfield and as a result play on a lush green ground. The only concession to being on an island in the middle of the Mediterranean is an artificial wicket.

Our regular wicket-keeper at the time was Alan who is sadly no longer with us. He had silky skills behind the stumps and it was unusual for a match to go by without him claiming at least one stumping victim. If we had a youngster playing against us and he was tempted out of his crease, as youngsters often are, Alan would always give him a life by deliberately missing the bails with his attempted stumping. Another difference between club cricket and Taverners cricket!

On this occasion, Alan was enjoying his cricket tour so much that he didn't want to spoil it all by actually playing cricket. Late into the night before the match, he and Iwan – an Ash Tree stalwart now retired from the rigours of the cricket field – had been chatting in the hotel bar to an elegant lady of a certain age. The following morning they checked with her in case they had said or done anything untoward. She said that on the contrary, she had enjoyed their company and that they had been "irresponsibly harmless".

This became our motto for the tour and indeed could serve as a maxim for most cricket tours. "Irresponsibly harmless" just about sums it all up. You may get some players doing something a bit silly on tour but it will rarely be detrimental to anyone but themselves.

Alan was enjoying himself in Menorca and was quite happy to give up his place to Geoff, who fancied a go at keeping wicket. Geoff was a friend of some of the players. He may well have played cricket in the dim distant past but certainly not recently. Whether he had ever kept wicket before was not clear.

The Menorca team seemed like a good bunch of guys, but gave the impression of being quite decent players. You can usually tell from the way a team warms up before a match as to how good they are going to be. In fact, just warming up at all before the game immediately put them in the upper quartile of teams that we play. Chatting about their recent fixture against the Warwickshire over 50s didn't help our confidence either. They won the toss and thankfully decided to bat. We didn't want the game over too quickly, however inviting the bar looked.

John, our opening bowler, was quite quick by Taverners standards. His first ball got some bounce off the artificial wicket and the batsman left it. The ball was still rising as it made minimal contact with the keeper's gloves and smashed straight into Geoff's face. He collapsed in a heap with blood streaming from his face.

He was helped off the field and Alan was roused from the comfort of his deck chair and San Miguel to don the pads. The cricket bit of Geoff's tour had lasted one ball (he wasn't required to bat). Although we were sorry about Geoff's misfortune, it has to be said that Alan's presence on the pitch brought a calm air of reassurance to the proceedings.

Wicket-keeper is a key position in cricket whether it's at Taverners or Test level. Ideally, you want your best glove man behind the stumps. This may seem obvious but has rarely happened for England since Jack Russell hung up his gloves in 1997. For the last ten years, Chris Read has been arguably England's best wicket-keeper. During that time, he has only played fifteen Tests but, despite that, he is the only keeper from any country, to claim six dismissals in an innings three times. This includes successive Test matches against Australia in 2006/07. England treated him rather badly, partly because it was perceived that his batting wasn't up to scratch, but mainly because he apparently didn't get on with Duncan Fletcher. 'Not getting on with' the England coach is not a good idea if you want to play for England. Interestingly, Read averages over 36 with the bat in all first-class cricket; his *bête noire*, Geraint Jones, slightly less. Matt Prior, a better bat than both of them, seems to have settled the argument for the time being now that his keeping has improved.

At the Ash Tree, we never had a selection dilemma with the wicket-keeping position. If Alan was available to play, he was the keeper. No one would argue with that. With his trademark leg glances and subtle cuts, he was also useful for some late order runs. With Alan in position behind the stumps, Menorca resumed their innings. They progressed at a steady rate with three of their batsmen retiring at 30. We felt we had done quite well to restrict them to 188 off their 30 overs.

Just over six an over was the asking rate which doesn't sound too much if you say it quickly. The trouble was that the target was six runs *every* over. If an over went by when we didn't get at least six runs, then the asking rate went up. And we didn't, so it did. Three run-outs didn't help the cause and we finished up some way short of the target on 120 for 8.

We had lost but not disgraced ourselves. Our hosts looked after us well, recommending places that we should try to visit during our remaining time on the island. On our return to England, we received a copy of the match report that Menorca CC had put in their local newspaper. It included the words: "Though Ash Tree may not be the finest (cricketing) side we have met this season, they are certainly one of the friendliest and their après cricket is without equal." We took this as the compliment that I think it was intended to be.

We don't question an opposition player's parentage when he comes out to bat. We only appeal when we think someone is actually out. We would rather spend a month on a desert island with Simon Cowell and Louis Walsh listening to X-Factor contestants, than claim a catch that we knew hadn't carried. (Actually, I'll probably have to check on that one.) We try to win, and sometimes we do, but if we lose it's not the end of the world (unless it's the Congleton Gnomads, then we can get a little bit upset.)

Back home, once Zimbabwe had finished their two-match series, another cricket tour was about to begin. The West Indian tourists had arrived. They had successfully defended the Wisden Trophy for twenty seven consecutive years. Ray Illingworth was the last England captain to hold the trophy in 1969. The West Indians arrived with Walsh and Ambrose leading their attack and Brian Lara restored to the side after a self imposed absence.

The Windies won the first Test comfortably by an innings and 93 runs. They had a first innings lead of 133 in the second Test at Lords. What could possibly go wrong? A combination of complacency from the West Indian batsmen and excellent seam bowling from Caddick, Gough and Cork saw the West Indies bowled out for 54 in the second innings. England needed 188 to win and they scraped home by two wickets, helped by an enterprising 33 not out from Dominic Cork. On the Friday, the second day of the Test match, 21 wickets fell in 75 overs. It is the only Test match out of over 1,500 Tests ever played where some part of all four innings took place on the same day.

The Third Test at Old Trafford was drawn. This was followed by a two-day defeat for the West Indies at Headingley, which included being bowled out for 61 in the second innings. Caddick, who always seemed to bowl better in the second innings of a match, got four wickets in an over. The tour management must have been tempted to ask a watching Viv Richards to swap his microphone for a bat and give the West Indies a hand. Even in his late forties, and not having played for a few years, he would undoubtedly have strengthened both the batting and more importantly the resolve of the West Indies team.

England clinched the series with a win at the Oval. It was a sorry way for Walsh and Ambrose to play their last Test matches in England. In a sense, the West Indies have never really recovered from that series. During the build-up to the final Test, Roger Harper, their coach at the time, said that the players were "very low" and were "just waiting for it to end". A sad comment on any cricket tour but somehow even sadder because it was the West Indies.

The Ash Tree tour to Menorca, on the other hand, was deemed a success. The weather had been glorious. We'd had a few beers and made some new friends. We had even played some cricket.

2. Aborigine tour of England, 1868

If a team of Aborigines toured England this year playing cricket against various clubs and counties, including the MCC at Lords, it would be a pretty extraordinary event. Imagine what it must have been like in 1868, for that is when it happened. An official Australian team had yet to tour England. The first Test match between England and Australia was still ten years away.

Charles Lawrence was the man responsible for making the tour happen. Lawrence was a professional cricketer who had led a peripatetic life before arriving in Australia with an England cricket team in 1861. His cricketing jobs had taken him from Merton in Surrey, to Perth in Scotland, back to London and then to Dublin.

While in Scotland, he had been the professional at the Perth cricket club. At the age of twenty, he had played for a Scotland Twenty-Two against William Clarke's celebrated All England XI at Edinburgh in May 1849. England won the match but Lawrence was the star of the show. He took all 10 wickets in England's second innings. His figures were 10 for 53, coincidentally exactly the same analysis as those of Jim Laker when he took all ten Australian wickets in the second innings at Old Trafford in 1956.

The England team that turned out against Scotland in 1849 contained many of the famous players of the day, including John Wisden and George Parr. When Lawrence bowled Nicholas Felix, one of England's leading batsmen, Felix was so impressed that he walked up to him, took a half-crown out of his pocket and said:

"Take this in remembrance of me." The true spirit of cricket! Perhaps Kevin Pietersen could be encouraged to do the same sort of thing when he is out to a particularly good ball? Or maybe Ricky Ponting could be persuaded to go up to a fielder after he has been run out and say: "Jolly good throw Gary. Here's a fiver to remember me by."

William Clarke's All England XI was a band of professional cricketers who toured the country playing wherever they could. Clarke was a very successful bowler taking over 2,000 wickets. Seemingly, his only fault was that he would continue to bowl himself for too long 'always expecting to get a wicket in his next over'. I'm sure we all know captains like that.

Richard Daft, the Nottinghamshire batsman and member of Clarke's team, wrote: "What fun we had in these matches to be sure! We would arrive early, breakfast on bread, cheese and bottled ale. Tom Forster would leave his umpire's post and come into the pavilion for more at the fall of each wicket."

Apart from the "arrive early", it seems very reminiscent of Taverners cricket today! It is good to know that these traditions go back such a long way.

Some years later, William Clarke helped to secure an appointment for Charles Lawrence as professional at the Phoenix Club in Dublin. It would be gratifying to be able to say that the future Ashes series arose out of his time at the Phoenix but that would be stretching things a bit too far.

In 1858, Lawrence captained an All Ireland XI at Lords. He took eight wickets against a team of English gentlemen (professionals were not allowed to play for the MCC at the time). Lawrence was an adventurer as well as a cricketer and he would have been interested in George Parr's plans to tour North America in 1859. Lawrence didn't make that trip but he was invited to be part of the 1861/62 tour of Australia that was led by H.H. Stephenson, the Surrey captain.

Around the same time, Charles Dickens was offered £10,000 to undertake a reading tour of Australia. His tours of North America had been interrupted rather inconveniently by the American Civil War. In the end, he didn't go but finished off *Great Expectations* instead; an appropriate theme for that first tour of Australia and indeed all subsequent ones.

Stephenson's England team sailed from Liverpool on 20th October in the *Great Britain*, arriving in Melbourne on Christmas Eve. The Australians embraced the visitors with open arms in 1861, much like they do today but possibly for different reasons. Unlike today, the Australians were not expecting to win every match. Links with the mother country were still very strong and any contact was welcome. 15,000 people turned up to watch the first game on New Year's Day at the Melbourne Cricket Ground.

To make the games more even, most of the Australian teams fielded twenty-two players, as in Twenty-Two of Victoria and Twenty-Two of Castlemaine. The tourists played twelve matches, but they were not classified as first-class. They won six and lost two, with four drawn. It was very much a goodwill tour with the Australian hospitality often overwhelming. William Caffyn wrote "Scarcely a day passed without our being entertained to champagne breakfasts, luncheons and dinners." In the circumstances, they did well to lose only two games!

In January 1862, they played a match at Sydney. The Secretary for Lands, John Robertson, controversially allowed the promoters to charge admission to the public while arranging a free stand for parliamentarians. Some things never change!

Towards the end of the tour, Stephenson's team divided for a match at the MCG that was billed as The World versus a Surrey XI and was designated as a first-class match. The six Surrey players were joined by five locals, who supposedly had Surrey affiliations, to form the Surrey XI. The World XI was made of the six non-Surrey tourists and another five locals. The World XI won by six wickets thanks to an impressive all-round performance by George Bennett who scored 72 and then took 7 for 30 and 7 for 85.

The tour was a great success and Charles Lawrence enjoyed himself so much that he accepted an invitation to stay on as professional cricket coach at the Albert Club in Sydney. He thought that there was money to be made in Australia and tried to persuade some of the other members of the team to stay on. However, they all sailed home to England leaving Lawrence with his dreams and plans.

He recorded in his diary that he had formed the idea of teaching the Aborigines cricket after seeing them throwing boomerangs and spears. He felt sure that, if he could take them to England, he would make his fortune.

Australia rather than North America became the preferred destination for cricket tours from England. George Parr brought another England team back to Australia in 1863/64 and the game really began to take off. Meanwhile in North America, baseball was establishing itself as the national game. If it hadn't been for the American Civil War, the development of cricket might have been very different.

Babe Ruth would probably have made a useful cricketer, but the Australians would have had a great time sledging a player whose first name was Babe and second name was Ruth. Joe DiMaggio was six years younger than Don Bradman and could have been a serious rival. I'm sure that Marilyn Monroe would have been welcomed at Lords, but obviously would not have been allowed in the Long Room.

Meanwhile, Charles Lawrence was pursuing his dream of taking an Aborigine team to England. Aborigines had been playing cricket for a few years and he got together a group of players with the intention of taking them to England. They had a number of warm up games before departing from Sydney on 8th February 1868. Also on board the ship to England was a much-travelled clergyman, Henry Nisbett, who wrote about his travels. His journal has daily entries from the time they left Sydney to when they docked at Gravesend on 13th May. At no point does he mention that there were thirteen Aborigines on board. Did he fail to notice them? Did he think they were not worth mentioning?

The only conclusion one can draw is that it reflects the narrow-minded thinking of some people at the time. It just wouldn't do to acknowledge the existence of some 'dark skinned' chaps on the same ship as him. Best to adopt the ostrich approach and pretend they aren't there. Maybe they would go away. It must have been very difficult for the Reverend, so far from home, to have the company of thirteen Aborigines on a three month boat journey. We can only hope that if he met them on board, they worked hard to put him at his ease.

All the Aborigines had 'nicknames' given to them by their original employers when they worked on the land in Australia. This was because the newly arrived white landowners struggled to pronounce their tribal names. Arrahmunijarrimun was, perhaps understandably, known as Peter. Jungunjinanuke acquired the name of Dick-a-Dick. Bripumyarrimin was known as King Cole. Pripumuarraman, aka Charley Dumas, was not much of a cricketer but gained his place in the squad because he was an expert with the boomerang. The star of the team was Unaarrimin, better known as Johnny Mullagh. Only injury prevented him from playing for the Victoria State side before the 1868 tour of England.

According to Lawrence's own diary, the Aborigines were very popular with other passengers on board. They drew pictures of animals and birds for the children and also made toys and other implements out of wood. Luckily, it seems that not everyone was as uptight as the Reverend.

Even so, Lawrence must have been concerned as they sailed up the Thames and docked at Gravesend. How would the team be received? Had enough games been arranged? How would the Aborigines handle the strange environment and new experiences? Would he make enough money to justify the trip?

Lawrence's partner, William Hayman was there to meet them. He had left Australia six weeks earlier in order to arrange the tour itinerary. He had good connections with Kent and this had helped him arrange some early games but the full tour was by no means agreed. Lawrence himself was well known at Surrey, having played for them before leaving for Australia. He also had some influence at the MCC through his earlier association with Ireland.

Using his contacts from Surrey and Ireland, Lawrence managed to persuade the MCC to play his team at Lords on the 12th and 13th of June. The success of his tour was then assured. Once the MCC agreed to play them, many other offers of games were forthcoming. In the end, the team played a total of forty seven matches, crisscrossing the country by train and carriage.

After only two weeks to acclimatise and get fit, the first ever touring side from Australia took on Surrey at the Oval. It was a strong Surrey side which batted first and scored 222 before an enthusiastic crowd of over 7,000. Johnny Mullagh took 3 for 100 off 52 overs and Lawrence bowled 49 overs taking 7 for 91. Four balls per over was the norm in those days, but nevertheless they were impressive figures.

The visitors each wore a different coloured sash that ran from the left shoulder to the right waist. The colours were printed on the scorecard so spectators could easily identify each player. Lawrence of course didn't need a distinguishing coloured sash.

On the second day, before an even bigger crowd, the Australians managed only 83 with Johnny Mullagh top scoring with 33. Following on, they did rather better scoring 132. Johnny Mullagh again top scoring with 73. Considering they had only been playing cricket for a few years and had to adapt very quickly to unusual English conditions (in every sense), the Aborigines had done remarkably well.

Johnny Mullagh had been the star with both bat and ball. After the match had finished, in a forerunner for future man of the match awards, he was presented with a gold sovereign, together with a watch and chain. A bit classier than the ubiquitous magnum of champagne and oversized cheque that gets handed out today.

During the lunch break on the first day, George Tarrant, one of England's top fast bowlers, took the opportunity to bowl at Mullagh in the nets. Charles Lawrence had been telling everyone how good he was and Tarrant wanted to test him out. At the end of a fifteen-minute net session, Tarrant walked up to Mullagh and said: "I have never bowled to a better batsman." Praise indeed!

After the game against Surrey, Lawrence and his team were invited to go to the Derby at Epsom. The crowd at the racetrack cheered them. Seemingly, the Aborigines encountered very little overt racism in England. There was curiosity from the general public and what today we would regard as racist comments but not hostility.

More insidious was the attitude of the press. *Bell's Life in London* had this article about the arrival of the team:

> "The Aboriginal black cricketers who make their appearance at the Oval next week are the first specimens of the Australian native we have seen in this country. They are veritable representatives of a race unknown to us until the days of Captain Cook and a race which is fast disappearing from the earth. If anything will save them it will be the cricket ball. Other measures have been tried and failed. The cricket ball has made men of them at last."

It presumably did not occur to the writer that the fact that the Aboriginal race was "fast disappearing" may have had something to do with the arrival of European settlers in Australia. They may have brought cricket with them but they also brought disease, destruction and discrimination to the Aborigines.

The Times was dismissive of the Australian team and after the first few games, barely mentioned them. The *Daily Telegraph* commented at the time that "Nothing of interest comes from Australia except gold and black cricketers." When the first official Australian touring party came to England in 1878, many of the spectators were surprised that the players were not black. Murdoch, Bannerman, Spofforth et al were no doubt not amused.

After the Epsom Derby, the team returned to the Oval for a day of sports and entertainment. 4,000 people turned up to watch. The Aborigines, dressed in traditional costume, started with a mock hunt. This was followed by a spear throwing display and then several of the team demonstrated their expertise with the boomerang.

The athletics events were keenly contested. A certain E. Ford of Lambeth won the 100 yards dash and the 440 yards race but the Aborigines won most of the other events. It is recorded[3] that after Bullocky (aka Bullchanach) won the throwing the cricket ball event with a throw of 105 yards, he was challenged by a nineteen-year-old W.G. Grace who was in the crowd. W.G., presumably without his distinctive beard at that point, beat him with a throw of 118 yards.

The other main attraction on the day, and at all subsequent matches, was Dick-a-Dick's ability to 'dodge' cricket balls. Armed with a parrying shield and leangle (an Aboriginal war club), Dick-a-Dick played 'dodge the ball'. For the price of a shilling, anyone could have a shy at him. Although standing no more than ten yards away, no one managed to hit him. He managed to parry or deflect every ball.

The tour moved south where a strong Kent side scored 298 against them. Mullagh again starred with 6 for 125 off 59 overs. It's a shame he's not around today to explain to England's bowlers how to complete so many overs and still stay fit. Fred Trueman would no doubt have approved. The Australians only managed 123 in reply with Dick-a-Dick scoring 27 to at least show that he could bat a bit as well as dodge cricket balls.

The next game was against Richmond at Deer Park and Johnny Cuzens (aka Zellanach) made his first major contribution. He took 5 for 28 off 23 overs to help dismiss Richmond for 74. He then top scored with 24 in the Australian's first innings total of 97. Richmond made a better fist of it in their second innings scoring 236 (Mullagh 4 for 65 and Cuzens 3 for 49). The Australians were 82 for 3 at the end of the last day and the match was drawn.

Despite taking a first innings lead against Sussex thanks to 63 from Lawrence and 39 from Mullagh, the Australians lost the match after collapsing in the second innings. It was becoming apparent

---

3 Alverstone and Alcock's *Surrey Cricket: Its History and Association.*

that they really only had three top class batsman – Lawrence, Mullagh and Cuzens. If they failed, then the team was in trouble.

The Australians moved on to Lewisham whom they beat to register their first win of the tour. This was a much-needed boost as their next match was to be the highlight of the tour – a game against the MCC at Lords.

In many ways, this was one of the most extraordinary cricket matches ever played. The visitors to Lords were a group of tribal Aborigines lead by a white Englishman (and not even an amateur at that!) The Aborigines were perceived as 'savages' by most of the country and referred to as "darkies" in the newspapers. Most of them had only been playing cricket for a few years. Nevertheless, there they were, in 1868, walking out at Lords to play an MCC team representing the English Establishment. Included in the team was the Earl of Coventry (MCC President in1859) and Viscount Downe (MCC President in 1872).

The MCC batted first and were all out for 164. Mullagh and Cuzens did the bulk of the bowling taking five and four wickets respectively. When the Australians batted, they were soon in trouble at 6 for 2 and then 43 for 4, but a brilliant 75 from Mullagh, supported by 31 from Lawrence, helped them to a first innings lead of 21. Cuzens bowled well when the MCC batted again, taking 6 for 65. Among his victims were an Earl, a Knight of the Realm and an Army Captain; quite an impressive hat trick! The Earl of Coventry was clean bowled for 0, Sir Frederick Hervey-Bathhurst was also clean bowled for 0 and Captain Trevor was bowled for 13.

At that point in this epic clash of cultures on the hallowed turf of Lords, it is fair to say that the Aborigines held the upper hand. They only needed to get 90 to achieve an historic victory. Unfortunately, things did not work out as they might have hoped.

First of all Bullocky, for no apparent reason, had failed to turn up on the second day. He was marked down in the score book as 'Absent ill . . .. 0'. It was never fully established what the problem was, but anyone who has been on a cricket tour can imagine the possible scenario. There you are at the bar drinking with your new mates, the Earl and the Viscount. They invite you on for a few more and before you know it, you are Brahms and Liszt and unable to get up in the morning. It could happen to anyone.

On top of this, Charles Lawrence was injured and had to have a runner. Almost inevitably there was a mix up and he was run out. Mullagh failed with the bat for once, Cuzens hit a brave 21 but the rest collapsed to the slow bowling of Charles Buller. The Australians were all out for 45 and the MCC had won.

The Aborigines had not disgraced themselves. Well, Bullocky had but I think he can be forgiven. After the match, Dick-a-Dick invited the MCC members to pay a shilling and try and hit him with a cricket ball. None succeeded and he walked away with a tidy sum.

The tour moved on with games in South Wales, Yorkshire and Lancashire. The team found themselves travelling very long distances due to the itinerary being put together as they went along. Invitations to play were accepted and games arranged on an ad hoc basis with the result that they criss-crossed the country, on one occasion travelling from Rochdale to Swansea and then back the next day to Bradford.

While in Yorkshire, they played the Gentlemen of Sheffield at Bramhall Lane. Sheffield batted first and scored 233 with Mullagh taking 6 for 95. The Australians replied with 185, of which Mullagh scored 55. The most remarkable event was achieved by Twopenny (aka Murrumgunarrimin) in his innings of 22. He managed to score nine runs (all run, with no overthrows) in one hit. There is no record in any cricket match of this ever having been achieved either before or since.

The cricket correspondent for the *Sheffield Independent* described Twopenny's extraordinary achievement:

"Twopenny made the sensational hit of the match, accomplishing a feat which has no parallel on Bramhall Lane, and we should say on no other ground. Mr Foster, who was well up, did not offer for some time to go for the ball and when he started it was at a slow pace. The result being that nine was run for the hit amidst vociferous cheering".

This wonderful description of the fielder saying that he "did not offer for some time to go for the ball and when he started it was at a slow pace" could have come from almost any Ash Tree CC match in recent memory. I've no doubt that it will also strike a chord with many other Taverners players around the country.

The Australians were now halfway through their tour. So far it had been a great success. The English public seemed to take to the Aborigine players. They played the game in a good spirit, applauding their opponents onto the pitch and were clearly enjoying themselves. Although the team relied heavily on their three top players, the rest were excellent fielders and always entertaining. However, one thing had occurred that depressed and disheartened the whole touring party. One of their players had been taken ill suddenly.

King Cole had played in every game up to and including the match at Lords. He played in the next game at Southsea but soon afterwards developed a heavy chest cold that rapidly got worse. The tour moved on to Bishop Stortford but Lawrence took King Cole to London for treatment. They went by train to Paddington and then took a cab to Guy's Hospital.

King Cole's chest cold developed into pneumonia. There were no antibiotics to counter pneumonia in 1868 and the indigenous Australians were particularly susceptible to such illnesses. So it proved for King Cole. His condition deteriorated and he died in hospital four days later on 24th June.

It was a terrible blow for Lawrence and his team but the tour had to go on. They continued moving around the country. They beat Tynemouth and drew with Northumberland, Middlesborough and then Scarborough. Johnny Mullagh almost single-handedly beat Bootle. He scored 51 in the first innings and then 78 in the second. He also took eleven wickets in the match.

He wasn't quite so successful with his boomerang display after the game. He threw his boomerang and a sudden gust of wind took it off course. Instead of coming back to him, it swooped over the crowd. One man did not duck in time and it hit him a resounding blow on the head. A doctor patched him up and all was well in the end.

Notwithstanding the boomerang incident, the Bootle captain presented Mullagh with fifty shillings after the game saying that he did not think that there was a better batsman in England.

The touring party moved south and had a return match against Sussex. The Australians did much better second time around and had the better of a drawn match. They also drew with Middlesex at Islington and with Surrey at the Oval again.

Twopenny had not been called upon to bowl much on the tour but he was let loose on East Hampshire at Southsea in the 43rd match. He had the remarkable figures of 9 for 9 in the first innings and 6 for 7 in the second. The opposition found his pace and hostility virtually unplayable. He bowled again in the next match against Hampshire and took 9 for 17 and 3 for 39. In two matches he had taken an incredible 27 wickets.

So why hadn't Lawrence used him earlier in the tour? The most likely explanation is that his action was a bit suspect and Lawrence didn't want to risk having him called for throwing early in the tour. If that had happened then it would have been bad publicity for the Australians and might have put future matches in jeopardy.

Twopenny became the first Aborigine to play first-class cricket on his return to Australia, when he played for New South Wales against Victoria in 1870. He failed to take a wicket in his 30 overs (0 for 56) and scored just eight runs. Although he was never called for throwing, it seems there was enough doubt to make it suspicious and he was not invited back to play.

There were just three matches to go on their tour of England. The Australians demolished a side from Reading. Mullagh got back in the action, taking 8 for 9 in the first innings and then went out and scored 94, the highest individual score on the tour. A draw against Godalming followed and then it was back to the Oval for one last game against Surrey.

John Constable Gregory, who had played twenty three first-class matches for Middlesex and Surrey, hit an undefeated 121, out of a Surrey total of 173. The Australians disappointed with the bat and were bundled out for 56 of which Bullocky top scored with 24. They batted much better in the second innings led by a fine knock of 63 from Johnny Cuzens, but Surrey only needed 27 to win which they scored, losing only one wicket.

The tour was over. The Australians had played forty seven games in 115 days. They had won 14, lost 14 and drawn the rest. The tour had been a financial success but none of the money went to the Aborigine players. They received no payment at all for the tour. On their return to Australia, they played a few games to wind down the tour and then the team dispersed.

As far back as 1860, the Central Protection Board for the Protection of Aborigines had been established in Victoria. In 1869, the State of Victoria passed the Aboriginal Protection Act. The word 'protection' was something of a euphemism. The Act gave the colonial Governor the power to control where each Aborigine lived, worked and carried out their business. The Board had wanted to stop the 1868 tour going ahead but did not have the statutory right to do so. Now they did.

Their argument was that they did not want Aborigines to be exploited. To an extent, the Aborigines that Lawrence took to England in 1868 were exploited by him. They received no payment for their efforts. The number of games they played and the huge amount of travelling involved must have been incredibly tiring. They had to put on a show after every game to demonstrate their native skills and entertain the English public.

And yet, and yet. They were welcomed everywhere they went. They were treated as equals in a way that they never were in their homeland either before they left or when they got back. They clearly enjoyed their cricket and showing off their skills with boomerang, spear and whips. And they got to play at Lords!

Of all the Aborigine players on the tour, Johnny Mullagh was the undoubted star. He was considered by many as the equal of any batsman in England at the time. He played in 45 of the 47 matches and scored 1,698 runs at an average of 23.65. This was at a time when any batting average over 20 was considered to be extremely good indeed. Many of the pitches were in a very poor state, and batting was significantly more difficult than it is today. He also bowled 1877 overs, taking 245 wickets at an average marginally over 10 apiece.

On his return, he joined Melbourne Cricket Club as a professional. For whatever reason, it didn't really work out for him. He only played six games, with moderate success, and he went back to his club side the following season. He scored so many runs for them that, nine years later, in 1879, he was picked to play for Victoria against Lord Harris's England side. He top scored in the second innings and the *Melbourne Argus* praised him for his "long reach, his cool artistic style, his judicious treatment of dubious balls and his vigorous drives".

Despite this performance, Mullagh was not selected for Victoria again. One can only speculate about the reasons for this. He went back to his job as a shearer and continued playing for his club side. In 1884, at the age of forty three, he was picked for a combined club side at the Adelaide Oval against Arthur Shrewsbury's England team. He scored 43 not out against an attack that included George Giffen, England's opening bowler at the time. Johnny Mullagh continued playing cricket until a few months before his death in 1891 at the age of fifty.

No Aborigine player, or player who acknowledged that he had Aborigine blood, represented Australia for the next one hundred years. At least three Aborigine players during that period were generally considered good enough to play for Australia – Alec Henry, Jack Marsh and Eddie Gilbert – but none of them did. The reason that they didn't was almost certainly due to overt racism in Australian society during that time. All three were 'no balled' at the height of their powers; in Gilbert's case, days after clean bowling Don Bradman in a Sheffield Shield match for a duck.

Many years later, in 1996, Jason Gillespie became the first male cricketer[4] who acknowledged his Aboriginal heritage to play for Australia. Gillespie's father is of Scottish, German and Aboriginal ancestry, while his mother has a Greek and Irish background. Gillespie did not make a big issue of his Aboriginal heritage but

4 Faith Thomas played for the Australian women's cricket team in 1958.

he did not deny it. It is believed that other players before him had Aborigine blood but could not admit it because of the prevailing prejudice of the time. Graeme Thomas toured South Africa in 1965/66 and there was some speculation at the time that he had Aborigine blood. South Africa would probably have refused him entry (as they did with D'Oliveria in 1969) and the Australian cricket authorities encouraged the thought that Graeme Thomas was of North American origin. Apparently that was acceptable to Mr Vorster and his cronies.

Jason Gillespie went on to become one of Australia's all time great bowlers. Only five players have taken more wickets for Australia than Gillespie[5] but he had a difficult time in the 2005 Ashes series and was dropped after the third Test. Gillespie returned to Australia and bounced back to be the leading bowler in the 2005/06 domestic season. He was selected to play in the two match series against Bangladesh and he made his mark in an impressive fashion.

In the First Test, Bangladesh won the toss and batted, scoring 427. When it was Australia's turn to bat, they were reduced to 93 for 6. Only a spectacular 144 from Adam Gilchrist saved the day. A gross injustice to Bangladesh you could say. Gillespie had the next highest score with 26. Second time around, Bangladesh only managed 148 and Australia were set 307 to win. A Ricky Ponting unbeaten century just about saw them home with three wickets to spare.

During the opening Test which was played at Fatullah, Australia's security manager had spotted, on closed circuit TV, a gunman in a black bandanna in the crowd. He rushed towards him only to discover that the man was in fact a member of the government's Rapid Action Brigade, assigned to protect the Australian team. A

---

5 Warne, McGrath, Lillee, Lee and McDermott have taken more wickets.

keen cricket lover, he had been using the telescopic sight on his rifle to get a better view.

In the second Test at Chittagong, a few days later, Bangladesh again batted first. Gillespie followed up his five wickets in the previous match by taking the first three wickets in four overs. Bangladesh were all out for 197 on the first day and Australia started their first innings. When Hayden was out just before the close, Gillespie was asked to go in as nightwatchman.

The use of a nightwatchman in cricket is a curious concept. The batting side loses a wicket near the end of the day and it is considered very important not to lose another one before the close of play. So, instead of sending in a player who can bat, is in the side for his batting and who presumably is best equipped to deal with the bowling and prevailing conditions, a lesser batsman is sent out. Quite often the nightwatchman is out before the close which of course completely defeats the object. Even if he survives, he is usually out quickly the next day or hangs around not making very many runs. Either way, the initiative is handed to the fielding side.

Steve Waugh didn't agree with the idea of a nightwatchman and did not use them when he was captain. Luckily for Gillespie, Waugh wasn't in charge in Bangladesh and so he got his chance. Gillespie had already shown his worth as a nightwatchman in October 2004 against India, when he had batted for four hours with Damien Martyn to help save the second Test in Chennai. In Bangladesh, he did even better.

Going in as nightwatchman in the second Test, at Chittagong, Gillespie batted for a total of nine and half hours. He achieved something that had eluded Ian Chappell, Mark Waugh, Colin Cowdrey and Mike Atherton to name but a few. On the 19th April 2006, his 31st birthday, he scored a Test double century. His 201 not out was an incredible innings. OK, it was against Bangladesh but it was still a Test match and the Australians had struggled to win the first match. Gillespie had never even scored a first-class century before, his top score being 58. Australia went on to win the game and Gillespie was named man of the series.

This chapter started with an extraordinary Aboriginal tour of England in 1868, featuring Johnny Mullagh scoring a majestic 75 at Lords. It ends with Jason Gillespie, scoring a double century in his 71st and final Test match for Australia. The facts and figure are amazing, the stories behind them even more so.

3. West Indies tour of England, 1984

David Gower versus Clive Lloyd. Arthur Scargill versus Margaret Thatcher. Winston Smith versus Big Brother. These were the epic battles of 1984.

Winston Smith sounds like he should have been a West Indian fast bowler. He would have had his work cut out to get into the West Indies side in 1984 with Holding, Marshall and Garner in the team. In fact the West Indies did call up Winston Davis, who was playing for Glamorgan at the time, to play one Test on that tour when Marshall was out injured. He was a good player but only appeared in fifteen Tests for the Windies because the fast bowling competition was so great. If Davis had not been available, Wayne Daniel was playing for Middlesex, or they could have called on a promising youngster in the tour party – Courtney Walsh.

England on the other hand had Derek Pringle and Jonathan Agnew. No surprise then that the West Indies arrived at Worcester for the tour opener in a confident mood.

1984 doesn't seem that long ago does it, but if you ask people under the age of forty about the Miners' Strike of that year, most of them will look blankly at you. It will ring a bell with some of them but few will know any details or appreciate its significance. It's the same with Larry Gomes. Didn't he play for Middlesex and then a few times for the West Indies?

Well yes, but Gomes actually played sixty Tests for the West Indies and had a batting average a fraction under 40. Together with

Gordon Greenidge, it was Larry Gomes who was the batting star of the 1984 tourists, not Viv Richards or Clive Lloyd or Desmond Haynes. He scored 400 runs in the series compared to Richards' 250.

Of course Sir Viv had his moments that summer. In the first One-Day International at Old Trafford he batted superbly to be 96 not out when the ninth wicket fell. Michael Holding joined him with the score at 166 for 9. In the last fourteen overs, Richards and Holding added 106 with Richards' share being 93. His score of 189 not out is still the fourth highest individual score in all ODIs.[6]

As with hazy recollections of the Miners' Strike and Larry Gomes, not everyone remembers that Eldine Baptiste played in all five Tests that tour or that Joe Gormley was the NUM President before Arthur Scargill. Joe Gormley allegedly worked for MI5 which is perhaps even more surprising than the fact that Baptiste bowled more overs than Michael Holding in the 1984 series. Eldine was a decent fielder too, as a startled Geoff Miller found out at Lords when he was run out at the bowler's end by an 80 yard throw from fine leg.

Baptiste did OK with the bat as well. His average of 34.8 was better than all the Englishmen in that series apart from Allan Lamb, and he was South African anyway. Younger readers who might be concerned by the recent presence of Pietersen and Trott in the England team may take some comfort in the fact that South Africans playing cricket for England is nothing new. Before Lamb

---

6 Sachin Tendulkar became the first player to score a double century in an ODI when he got 200 not out against South Africa in February 2010. Charles Coventry with 194 not out for Zimbabwe against Bangladesh (Zimbabwe lost!) and Saeed Anwar with 194 for Pakistan against India are the other players to have beaten Sir Viv's score.

there was Basil D'Oliviera and the one and only Tony Greig, and afterwards came Robin Smith.

Smith's older brother Chris and Greig's younger brother Ian also played for England. It's just a shame that we couldn't have got Barry Richards or Graeme Pollock or Mike Proctor. If you are going to have South Africans playing for England you might as well have the best. As *The Times* editorial put it when Barry Richards was in his pomp: "Is there no way in which Richards of Hampshire could be co-opted into the English Test side? Can no patriotic English girl be persuaded to marry him? He is quite personable. Failing that, could not some elderly gentleman adopt him?"

As it happened, it was just as well that Allan Lamb was turning out for England in 1984. He got centuries in three successive Tests, the first batsman to do this for England since Ken Barrington in 1967. All the other English batsmen that series made heavy weather of the West Indies attack, although Graeme Fowler got a brave century at Lords in the Second Test.

Ask anyone when the last pitched battle to be fought on English soil was and, if they are still there by the time you have finished the question, they might say the Battle of Sedgemoor in 1685. That was when the Duke of Monmouth, Charles II's illegitimate son, landed on the Dorset coast and unsuccessfully tried to seize the throne from James II on the grounds that he was a Catholic. If they know their history well, they might say the Battle of Clifton (Cumbria not Bristol) in 1745. This was a preliminary engagement prior to the Battle of Culloden the following year. A real 'clever clogs' might say the Battle of Bossenden in 1838 when the self-styled Sir William Courtenay, claimed to be the Messiah (see later reference to Arthur Scargill). He preached to the poor rural labourers of Kent that if they followed him he would lead them to a land of paradise. They were simple folk and had little to lose but their lives, which a number of them did when the army was called out to suppress the uprising.

Sedgemoor, Clifton, Bossenden are all good answers but all wrong. On 18th June 1984 just as West Indies were putting the finishing touches to their victory in the First Test at Edgbaston, thousands of police fought a pitched battle with thousands of miners at the Battle of Orgreave in South Yorkshire.

Brutal force, overwhelming odds, battered heads, glimmers of hope relentlessly crushed, desperate self defence to avoid serious injury, yes, Edgbaston in 1984 was not a happy place for English cricketers.

Gower won the toss and felt obliged to bat first because he had two spinners in the side. He soon regretted his decision. Garner immediately had Fowler caught behind for a duck. This brought Derek Randall to the wicket rather sooner than he probably would have wanted. Randall was not afraid of fast bowling, as his epic 174 against Dennis Lillee in the Centenary Test had shown, but that had been seven years before and now he was exposed rather too early to the West Indian pace attack. Randall was more vulnerable early in his innings than most batsmen. Joel Garner soon bowled him, also for a duck, and England were 5 for 2.

Andy Lloyd, who was making his Test début on his home ground, had opened with Graeme Fowler. The benefit of familiarity with the ground was probably outweighed by having to face Garner, Marshall and Holding in your first match for your country. He played soundly for a while but then was hit on the head by a short ball from Marshall. He spent the rest of the match in hospital and never played Test cricket again.

Gower came in and scored a very elegant 10. Only some lusty blows from Botham and sensible batting from Downton enabled England to reach 191. After centuries from Gomes and Richards, the West Indies were on the ropes at 455 for 8. Then, a ninth wicket partnership between Baptiste and Holding helped the Windies to a final total of 606. Holding, in the side for his bowling, hit four sixes and eight fours in his innings of 69.

One curiosity from the debacle of England's bowling was that Derek Pringle, a medium pacer, bowled eighteen no balls. Very strange. The other oddity was David Gower not calling on Geoff Miller, England's fifth bowler, until the West Indies had scored 260. Maybe Gower had forgotten that he was a bowler? Or that he was on the field at all?

With Andy Lloyd unable to bat in the second innings, Paul Downton opened in his place and hit a courageous 56 but England soon subsided for 235 and the West Indies had no need to bat again. While all this was going on in Birmingham, the police and miners were squaring up to each other at the Battle of Orgreave.

Was it really a battle? I think if you asked the people that were there, they would probably say yes. The Messiah (aka Arthur Scargill) was present, leading his men. Attila the Hen (aka Margaret Thatcher) wasn't actually at Orgreave but she was there in spirit. Her troops were lined up like Roman legions with the police bashing their riot shields with their truncheons as they advanced. Like in *Gladiator* (and *Billy Elliot* for that matter), they parted to let the mounted police through to disperse the mass pickets.

There were many injuries on both sides. After the battle, ninety-five miners were charged with riot, unlawful assembly and similar offences. A number of the miners were eventually taken to court in 1987, but the trials collapsed and all charges were dropped.

Taking into account the fact that they were both happening in England at around the same time, you could not really get a greater contrast between the Battle of Orgreave and the rarefied atmosphere of a Test match at Lords. True, both were confrontations with a lot at stake; it's just that one had cucumber sandwiches at tea time and the other didn't. The other difference was that David Gower and Clive Lloyd would share a beer at the end of the day when hostilities were over, which is maybe where Margaret Thatcher and Arthur Scargill went wrong.

The miners' strike seemed to be the last thing on people's minds at Lords as a full house settled down to watch the Second Test. The match started encouragingly for England. A century stand between débutant Chris Broad (father of Stuart) and Graeme Fowler gave them a great start. Although their final total of 286 looked slightly below par, an inspired Ian Botham ensured a first innings lead of 41. He took 8 for 103 in 27.4 overs, his best ever Test figures. A solid unbeaten century by Lamb and a robust 81 from Botham in the second innings, saw England to a 328 lead at the end of the fourth day. Lamb had come off for bad light even though he was batting well. He had looked up in vain at an empty England balcony for some guidance from his captain. Gower later admitted in his autobiography that he had been watching the tennis at Wimbledon on television.

I took a greater than usual interest in the proceedings as I had a ticket for the last day. Viv Richards had always been a hero of mine but I had never seen him bat in the flesh. Now at last I would, and at Lords too!

Lamb was out straightaway the next morning and England added just 13 before David Gower declared. The West Indies were set 342 to win in five and a half hours. There was a great sense of anticipation in the crowd as Greenidge and Haynes went out to bat.

The West Indies had to score more in the fourth innings than had been scored in any of the other three innings. All results were possible with a draw favourite and an England victory a distinct possibility. A West Indies win wasn't really on the cards but at least we would get to see Viv Richards and Clive Lloyd bat.

With the score on 57, Haynes slipped after being sent back by Greenidge and was run out. This was the first time the West Indies had lost a wicket in the second innings for seven successive Tests. The fall of wicket brought Larry Gomes to the crease.

Gomes did not have the power or dashing stroke play of the typical Caribbean player but he did have a sound technique and a wonderful temperament. His undemonstrative style offered a balance to the flair of the other batsmen in the team. He was the 'glue' that invariably held the innings together.

I was just hoping that he wouldn't stick around too long this time. The West Indies still had most of the day to bat. I was looking forward to seeing Viv Richards stride out at Lords and hopefully score a century. This would be followed by a West Indian collapse and an England victory.

None of these things happened. The West Indies didn't lose another wicket. Gordon Greenidge powered his way to an unbeaten double century at nearly a run a ball. Gomes, giving him the strike wherever possible, ended up on 92 not out.

My recollection is that I was more upset at not seeing Richards bat than about England's defeat. You shouldn't be too unhappy when you've seen Greenidge hit one of the great Test innings but it would have been nice to see Viv bat, even if it was just a cameo at the end!

David Gower, in his second Test match as England captain, became just the fourth Test captain in history to lose after declaring. From time to time, Botham enjoys reminding him of this when they are commentating for *Sky*. Gower, not unreasonably, retorts that he wasn't the one bowling. (Botham followed up his 8 for 103 in the first innings with 0 for 117 off 20.1 overs in the second.)

It's always one of the pleasures at a Test match to wander round the ground when the game is not on. Some people do it even when the cricket is being played which always seems a little odd to me. After the match had finished, my friends and I strolled round Lords, soaking up the atmosphere, reflecting on the day's play and doing some 'people watching'.

We spotted a group of West Indian players who had not been playing in the match, including Richie Richardson. I went over to ask for his autograph and the players with him laughingly made the point repeatedly that he was Richards' son. From the look on Richie Richardson's face, it wasn't the first time he had heard the joke.

Two down and three to play. The teams met again at Leeds for the Third Test. After scoring 0 and 6 in the Texaco Trophy one-dayers, Mike Gatting hadn't been picked for the First Test. He was brought back for the Second Test and, after scoring 1 and 29, he was dropped again. So he wasn't at Headingley which is a shame because it is pretty close to Orgreave and he could have gone along to see how the Miners' strike was getting on and to witness firsthand the demonstrations, or 'a few people singing and dancing'[7] as he might have described them.

England batted first and scored 270, with Lamb getting the second of his centuries. It seemed a modest total but there was the bonus of Malcolm Marshall sustaining a double fracture of the left thumb. He was only able to bowl six overs and it was announced that he would take no further part in the match.

When the West Indies batted, Bob Willis had Greenidge caught in the slips and Paul Allott got Haynes and Richards cheaply, to leave the tourists in a precarious state at 78 for 3. Not for the last

---

7 See Mike Gatting's description of the protests in South Africa to the England 'rebel' tour of 1990.

time, Gomes came to their rescue. Partnerships with first Lloyd then Dujon took the score to 200. Baptiste and Harper were then both out for ducks but, just as it looked as though England might finally get the upper hand, Holding came in and hit a savage 59 including five sixes.

Garner was run out trying to give Gomes, who was on 96, the strike. As the players prepared to leave the field, Marshall came out with his left wrist in a plaster. Gomes took the opportunity to reach his century by hitting Willis over his head for a boundary. Marshall managed to hit a four one-handed, to the third man boundary before edging Allott to Botham at slip.

Marshall's boundary took the West Indies past 300. This was irritating for England but at least he wouldn't be able to bowl with a broken thumb and his left wrist in plaster .... would he?

Ten minutes later, England had the answer to that question. Marshall opened the bowling and soon had Chris Broad caught off a ball that rose viciously. Paul Terry was England's latest answer to the troubled No.3 spot. He had scored five centuries for Hampshire that season but followed up his 8 in the first innings with only a single in the second. The gap between county and Test cricket was considerable, especially when it was the West Indies that England were playing.

Marshall took two more wickets, including Graeme Fowler, who he caught and bowled one handed, to leave England on the verge of defeat at 135 for 6. In those days there was no play on Sundays, and when they resumed on Monday morning Marshall took all four remaining wickets to finish with his best ever Test figures of 7 for 53. The West Indies knocked off the required runs for the loss of two wickets and they had retained The Wisden Trophy yet again.

To make the West Indian bowlers even more intimidating, many of those playing in the 1980s and 90s were not only very quick, they were also very tall. Garner was 6' 8", Holding 6' 4" and later Walsh and Ambrose came in at 6' 6" and 6' 7" respectively. England seem to be going down the same road. If Tremlett, Broad and Finn ever make up the attack together, their average height will be 6' 7". You don't have to be tall to be a fast bowler though. Fred Trueman and Harold Larwood, who would be in most people's Top Ten fast bowlers of all time, were both well under 6'. Frank Tyson, one of the fastest bowlers ever, was 5' 7" in his socks. Of all the formidable fast bowlers playing in the West Indies heyday, Malcolm Marshall was arguably the best, and he was less than 6' tall.

England still had pride to play for and, at Old Trafford in the Fourth Test, they once again had the West Indies in early trouble at 70 for 4. Paul Allott, on his home ground, bowled well, taking three of the wickets. Greenidge was still there though and together with the wicket-keeper Jeffrey Dujon proceeded to put on 197 for the fifth wicket.

Dujon played eighty one Tests for the Windies over a ten year period. He was an elegant batsman and good enough to hold down the No.6 position in the team. This was important as it allowed the West Indies to play four fast bowlers and Roger Harper. On this occasion, Dujon reached his century but was out just before the close of play on the first day. This brought Winston Davis in as nightwatchman.

Despite his seven wickets with a broken thumb, Marshall had accepted medical advice and was not playing in this game. Davis had taken his place and, as the new boy, had been given the nightwatchman duties. At 267 for 5, the match was reasonably balanced. All England had to do was get rid of Davis as soon as possible the next morning and then 'clean up the tail'.

It didn't quite work out like that. Davis chose this moment to score an entertaining and career best 77. Gordon Greenidge went on to complete his second double century of the series and the West Indies were all out for exactly 500.

When England batted, Lamb scored his third successive hundred, and he had Paul Terry to thank for it. Terry had retired hurt when a short ball from Winston Davis hit him and broke his arm. When the ninth wicket went down, Lamb was on 98 not out. As the players began to leave the field, David Gower waved them back on.

Like some young lieutenant in the First World War urging his troops out of the trenches on to the field of battle, Gower ushered Paul Terry on to the pitch. His left arm was plastered and in a sling. Lamb was due to face the next over. England needed 23 to avoid the follow-on. Lamb needed 2 for his century.

Thinking that Terry had come out simply to allow him to get his century, Lamb played the first five balls defensively then took 2 runs off the last ball. He tucked his bat under his arm and once again the players started to come off the field of play. Once again, Gower waved them back on to continue the fight. Presumably, having seen Marshall bat one-handed in the previous Test, Gower was trying to emulate his heroics. Or rather, he was hoping that Paul Terry would.

Terry had to face the next over from Garner. He had struggled against him when he had two good arms. How he was supposed to play him with one arm in a sling was anyone's guess. Predictably enough Garner cleaned bowled him second ball. It was early days in Gower's captaincy but maybe he was modelling himself a bit too closely on Paul Newman in *Cool Hand Luke*. I think what we had here was a failure to communicate.

England collapsed in the second innings and were all out for 156. Roger Harper, built like a fast bowler but actually a slow off spinner, took six wickets. Paul Terry was not asked to make the sacrifice a second time and, like Andy Lloyd, never played Test cricket again.

England had many problems in the series but the No.3 slot was one of the biggest. So far, Derek Randall had scored 0 and 1. David Gower had given it a go for one Test and scored 3 and 21. Finally, Paul Terry had scored 8 and 1 followed by 7 and 'absent injured'. Seven innings totalling 41 runs at an average of just under 6.

The West Indies No.3, Larry Gomes, on the other hand, over the same four Tests, had scored 143, 10, 92*, 104*, 2* and 30. A contribution of 381 runs at an average of 127. A huge difference that goes a long way to explaining why England had lost all four Tests so far.

Where was Graham Gooch when you needed him? Well Goochie was still playing, indeed at the age of thirty-one, he was in his prime. While England were facing the ferocious West Indian attack, Gooch was scoring over 2,000 runs for Essex in the County Championship, at an average of 69. He wasn't playing for England because he was not available for selection. In 1982, he had captained an English team to South Africa on a rebel tour.

It was a pretty good team. Boycott, Amiss, Underwood, Hendrick, Emburey, Knott et al but most of the team were past their best. Gooch was different. He would have been an automatic selection for England. The same could not really have been said of any of the other players. So why did he go? Money, a naive belief that what he was doing was OK and money. He probably did not anticipate a three-year ban either.

England could not call upon Gooch so they turned to the next best thing, Chris Tavare. He was having a moderate season for Kent and was unlikely to set the pulse racing when he went out to bat, but at least he would not sell his wicket cheaply. With a bit of luck, he might irritate the West Indians and also slow things down a bit by walking halfway to square leg and back after each delivery.

So, that was the batting sorted out, what to do about the bowling? Many of the bowlers used by England in the series – Willis, Pringle, Cowans, Foster, Cook, and Miller – were either injured or dropped. The selectors stuck a pin in the county averages and came up with Jonathan Agnew and Richard Ellison.

England had lost four Tests in a row and no English team had ever lost a home series 5 – 0. Could they avoid the dreaded 'whitewash' or, as the banner at the Oval famously proclaimed, 'blackwash'?

Clive Lloyd won the toss and chose to bat. England's new bowling attack soon had the West Indies at 70 for 6. Had the selectors hit upon the magic formula by a lucky accident? Lloyd led a minor (no pun intended) recovery with 60 not out but his team were all out for 190, their lowest score of the series. Ian Botham, well supported by Allott and Ellison, had got five wickets and in the process joined Bob Willis and Fred Trueman on the 300 Test wicket mark.

Chris Broad was out just before the close and Surrey off spinner Pat Pocock, having scored 0 and 0 in the previous Test, was offered up as a sacrificial nightwatchman. He survived the evening session and lasted forty-six minutes the next morning before being out for another duck. Prior to his dismissal, he was on the receiving end of a persistent short pitched barrage that did neither the West Indies nor the umpires any credit.

The Laws of Cricket at the time, as they do still, quite clearly state that "The bowling of short-pitched balls is unfair if, in the opinion of the umpire at the bowler's end, it constitutes an attempt to intimidate the striker". The laws go on to say "The relative skill of the striker shall also be taken into consideration." The sanctions of 'no ball', 'final warning' and ultimately not allowing the bowler to continue for the rest of the innings were all in place in 1984.

For forty-six minutes, Pocock was protecting himself first and his wicket second. It might seem quite entertaining if you are a West Indian supporter but it was against both the spirit and the laws of cricket. "The relative skill of the striker shall also be taken into consideration." Pat Pocock played in twenty five Tests and averaged just over 6 with the bat. He played 554 first-class games and averaged 11. Pocock was a tailender. It would have been very easy for the umpire to say to the bowler 'if you bowl another short pitch ball, I will no ball you.' The umpires, David Constant and Barrie Meyer, chose not to take this simple action.

It's always difficult to complain about something when you are getting hammered, and England did not make too much fuss but there is a picture in the 1985 edition of *Wisden* that sums it up. The heading is 'The Unacceptable Face of Test Cricket'. It is a photograph of Pocock avoiding a bouncer from Marshall. One foot is off the ground pointing towards square leg. His bat is in the air pointing towards third man and his head is jerked sideways pointing down to fine leg. It is not a picture of a batsman. It is a picture of someone bravely trying to avoid being carried off the pitch to hospital.

Maybe the West Indies were upset because they had been bowled out for under 200? Perhaps their many supporters at the Oval got them going? Maybe they were just being macho? Whatever the motivation, it worked. England were bowled out for 162. Graeme Fowler negotiated the short-pitched onslaught for a time but eventually was hit on the arm and had to leave the field. He came back later and top scored with 31. No one else got over 20.

When the West Indies batted for a second time, they were once again in trouble early on. Jonathan Agnew joined the party and claimed Greenidge and Richards as his first Test victims. Gomes had a rare failure and the Windies were 69 for 3. Almost inevitably, as had happened in all the previous Tests, someone came to their rescue. This time it was Desmond Haynes. He had scored only 100 runs in the series up to that point but he got his head down for seven hours and played with a straight bat. His century, coupled with an entertaining 49 from Dujon, helped his side to a total of 346.

England needed to score 375 to win or bat for ten hours to draw. Neither seemed achievable based on the evidence of the first innings. It was clear which option Tavare had gone for when he occupied the crease for over three hours in scoring 49. Chris Broad also hung around for nearly three hours for his 39. Michael Holding then decided to come off his full run for the first time that summer and promptly blew away England's middle order. There was time for Botham to hit a quick fire 50 and Pocock to collect his fourth successive duck and England were all out for 202.

England had been 'blackwashed', bushwhacked, beaten and bruised. The 1984 West Indies team were undoubtedly a very good team but there was something slightly unedifying about the manner of their victory. Two England players had ended up in hospital never to play Test cricket again. Most of the time, short-pitched bowling was the rule rather than the exception. Physical intimidation was the order of the day with the ball frequently aimed at the England batsman rather than at their wicket. And the worst thing of all was that our bowlers couldn't do it back to them!

Pringle strived to get his pace above military medium and ended up bowling eighteen 'no balls' in an innings. Bob Willis was coming to the end of his career and could no longer muster the sustained hostility he was capable of in his younger days. When Botham, Allott and Ellison did manage to get amongst the West Indian batsmen, it was achieved by intelligent use of seam and swing not by bowling at their heads

The umpires of the day seemed unwilling or unable to enforce the laws of the game and restrict the use of short-pitched bowling. Robin Marlar, writing in the *Sunday Times* at the end of the tour, gives due credit to the West Indians. They were well led by Clive Lloyd, their batting had depth and reliability and their fast bowlers were controlled and penetrative. He examines England's weaknesses but also speculates how the West Indian batsmen, or indeed any batsmen, would have coped with the West Indies attack. He concludes by saying that the essence of cricket is the defence of the stumps by the batsman, not the defence of the body and that, in his opinion, the way the West Indies team was playing was deeply offensive to the spirit of cricket.

Eventually, a specific law had to be brought in to deal with short-pitched bowling. First of all a 'maximum of one bouncer per over' rule was experimented with and then the 'two bouncers per over' rule, which we still have today, was established. Although some fast bowlers may disagree, this seems to work. Persistent bowling of bouncers is either dangerous, if aimed at the head, or a negative tactic if continually passing above the head. A bouncer is far more effective as a surprise weapon.

So, in the battles of 1984, Clive Lloyd had unequivocally prevailed over David Gower. I don't want to spoil it for those who haven't read *Nineteen Eighty-Four* but Big Brother gives Winston Smith a right going over. Margaret Thatcher's 'victory' over Arthur Scargill was perhaps not so clear cut. She was triumphant but Scargill always claimed that "the greatest victory in the strike was the struggle itself."

We can only hope that the miners and their families who suffered twelve months of poverty and hardship agreed with him. The strike eventually ended in March 1985. Thatcher had defeated the so called 'enemy within'. Many of the pits were closed and communities destroyed. Manufacturing industry continued to decline and Britain became a haven for bankers and estate agents. At least the economy was safe in the hands of the financial sector. What could possibly go wrong?

Big Brother, Margaret Thatcher and Clive Lloyd all won in 1984 but it's not always winning that is important, it's how you win. If you win but in the process humiliate your opponent, does that not tarnish the victory? Watching proper batsmen face fast bowlers is one of the pleasures of Test cricket. Sometimes the batsman wins – Roy Fredericks against Dennis Lillee and Jeff Thomson at Perth in 1975. Michael Atherton taking on Allan Donald at Trent Bridge in 1998. Kevin Pietersen versus Brett Lee at the Oval in 2005. Sometimes the bowler wins – Curtly Ambrose against the Australians at Perth in 1992. Devon Malcolm destroying the South Africans at the Oval in 1994.

When the fight is even, it is great to watch. When it is a hapless tailender like Pocock being subjected to continuous intimidatory bowling deliberately aimed at his body, it is tantamount to bullying.

Overall, the tour had been a great success for the West Indies. They had won all five Tests, and were unbeaten in all other first-class matches. The only game they lost on the tour was the second One-Day International when, amazingly, Derek Pringle was man of the match with 3 for 21 off 10 overs.

The Pocock incident was undoubtedly a blemish, as was the West Indies Cricket Board's refusal to agree to a minimum number of overs in the day. Before the ICC had the power to regulate such things, it was up to the Boards of both countries to agree the conditions of play. The result in 1984 was that the West Indies maintained an average over rate of below fourteen overs an hour throughout the series. England had a similar over rate but they can be excused because of the time they spent looking for the ball after it had been dispatched by Greenidge, Gomes, Richards and even on occasions, Holding.

England did not have long to wait for the chance of redemption. They were scheduled to tour the West Indies in the winter of 1985/86. Revenge is a dish best served cold, apparently. Unfortunately for Gower and his team, it is particularly hot in the West Indies at that time of year.[8]

---

8 England suffered a 'blackwash' once again, losing the Test series 5 – 0. As in 1984, they had a single ODI victory as a consolation.

4. Australia tour of India, 2001

There are some songs that, when you first hear them, make such an impression that you just have to listen to them again, immediately. I'm not talking about songs that make you think, 'that's good, I wouldn't mind hearing that again.' There are plenty of songs like that. No, these are songs that obsess you for days on end.

It doesn't happen very often but when it does, it temporarily takes over your life. A lot of people tend to associate 'special' songs with other significant things that happen in their life. The songs I am referring to are rarely influenced by outside factors or special events. They just happen. One day you are going about your business and the next, you can't get the song out of your head.

It's a very personal thing. Others may like the song but not necessarily share the same fixation. Over the years, I have been afflicted every now and then by this obsession. *Mr Big* by Free, *I'll Be Your Lover Too* by Van Morrison, *Last To Die* by Bruce Springsteen and *La Cienega Just Smiled* by Ryan Adams are a few that have made their mark.

I have the same thing with certain cricketers which I will come to in a moment but first there is Bob Dylan to deal with. The best way to appreciate Dylan is to listen to whole albums. Why would you want to pick out one particular song from *Blood On The Tracks* or *John Wesley Harding* when they are all brilliant? With the advent of CDs, iPods, iTunes, Spotify and the rest, there is an increasing tendency for people to listen to individual tracks only. CDs and iPods are marvellous, of course they are, but some things have been lost with the demise of vinyl.

There are lots of great Dylan songs but only one has really grabbed me in the 'obsessional' sense. This may have something to do with the fact that it wasn't released on an album so it has to be listened to in isolation. Not only was it not released on an album, it wasn't finished, has never been performed by Dylan and was only recorded once.

The decision by Todd Haynes to call his 2007 film about Bob Dylan *I'm Not There* was inspired. The sound track CD of the film features covers of Dylan songs and contains just one song by Dylan himself – the "legendary, never-released, never-completed song" *I'm Not There.* At last the song had been officially released and everyone had the chance to listen to it, obsessively or otherwise.

I have the same mild fixation with certain cricketers. As with the songs, there is a distinction between players that I have enjoyed watching and reading about and players that I have a slightly unhealthy interest in.

It started with D.E.V. Padgett. I never saw him play but he was the only member of the Yorkshire team in the 1960s who had three initials. His name and initials resonated with me in some strange way and I would always check the Yorkshire scorecard to see how he had got on before looking for G. Boycott, D.B. Close, J.G. Binks and the rest.

The V stands for Vernon and many years later I would play cricket in the same team as a West Indian called Vernon. D.E.V. Padgett (even now it would seem presumptuous to refer to him as Doug) was most definitely not a West Indian. Born and bred in Bradford, he made his début for Yorkshire in 1951 at the age of 16. He was selected for a couple of Tests but never quite made the grade. He continued to play for the county of his birth for twenty years before retiring in 1971 to become Yorkshire's coach.

When he was a child, Michael Vaughan turned up to watch Yorkshire playing at Sheffield. During the tea interval, he was playing on the outfield with his friends when Doug Padgett spotted him and approached him about joining the county. Vaughan was born in Manchester, and at the time Yorkshire had a strict policy of only picking players that were born in Yorkshire (unless your name happened to be Lord Hawke.) Years later, when the rule was removed, Padgett checked up on the young Vaughan and offered him a place at the Yorkshire academy.

If Padgett hadn't recognised the latent talent, maybe Vaughan wouldn't have played first-class cricket, wouldn't have captained his country and maybe England would not have won the Ashes in 2005. It's all down to D.E.V. Padgett. Even now, when looking at a Yorkshire scorecard of the 1960s, I am drawn to Padgett's name and have to check how he got on. I would like to stress that I don't look at old Yorkshire scorecards all the time. Just every now and then.

Merely having three initials isn't sufficient. M.J.K. Smith never really did it for me. The M.J.K. really only distinguished him from all the other Smiths. K.W.R. Fletcher was always Keith Fletcher or sometimes even Fletch. The Headingley crowd called him other things when he was selected ahead of P.J. (Phil) Sharpe and dropped three difficult chances in the slips on his début against the Australians in 1968.

When Isaac Vivian Alexander Richards started to play for Somerset and the West Indies, all my prayers were answered. Not only did he have three initials, including a V, he was an absolutely wonderful player. For a number of years he was possibly the coolest man on the planet. When I.V.A. Richards came out to bat, the cricket ground was his stage and all the other players merely the supporting cast.

His brilliant career was preordained. He had an older brother, D. Richards, who played five first-class games and a younger brother, M. Richards, who played just one. It was Viv who was given the three initials and, although his mother apparently thought his brother Mervin was a more talented player, it was Viv who went on to play 121 Test matches and become a legend in his own lifetime.

Although I had other favourites over the years, it wasn't until V.V.S. Laxman came along that I had a player to really obsess about again. It was in 2001 that V.V.S. Laxman first burst into my consciousness. There was something incredibly exotic about his name and initials. Not just one V but two, and an S thrown in for good measure. To add to his mystique, his surname had an X in it. Not many cricketers can say that. Good game to play at a Test match when rain stops play: Ted Dexter, Martyn Moxon, Roger Prideaux, Paul Nixon. There must be more?

As well as having an exotic surname and wonderful initials, Vangipurappu Venkata Sai Laxman is also a sublime cricketer. He made an indelible mark on Test cricket during the Australian tour of India in 2001.

The Australian team, led by Steve Waugh, arrived in India with fifteen successive victories behind them. Seemingly they were unbeatable, vying with the 1948 Australians to be called the Invincibles, but they needed a series win in India to really prove themselves. No Australian team had won a series in India for thirty-one years.

Two days before the First Test in Mumbai, Sir Don Bradman died. Steve Waugh promised that the Australians would perform in a way that would make 'the Don' proud. Waugh won the toss and took a chance by inviting India to bat first. The pitch was a good one and putting India in meant that Australia would have to bat last on it.

Waugh's faith in his bowlers was rewarded. India were bowled out for 176, with only Tendulkar making a significant contribution. When Australia batted, they also struggled. They collapsed to 99 for 5 and it looked like Steve Waugh's gamble had failed. Three hours later, they were in a commanding position.

Adam Gilchrist joined Matthew Hayden and proceeded to smash 122 off 112 balls, including fifteen fours and four sixes. The Indian bowlers had no answer to his aggressive sweeping and pulling. Hayden cast aside his early circumspection and joined in the fun. He reached his century one over after Gilchrist.

India didn't do much better second time around. Once again only Tendulkar batted with any confidence before he was out to a diving catch from Ponting. Australia only needed 47 to win and the openers knocked them off by the end of the third day.

Australia moved on to Kolkata one up in a three match series. They had won their sixteenth successive match and looked likely to be the first Australian team to win a Test series in India since Bill Lawry's side in 1969/70. This probability seemed a certainty after they scored 445 despite a Harbhajan Singh hat trick that included the hero of the First Test, Adam Gilchrist, first ball.

The certainty looked like a foregone conclusion when India were shot out for 171 and invited to follow on. V.V.S. Laxman top scored with 59 off 83 balls and was rewarded by being promoted to his favourite position of No.3.

Both V.V.S. Laxman's parents were doctors and it had been assumed that he would follow them into the medical profession. Luckily an uncle spotted his talent and cricket won the day in the end. It would take a modern miracle from Laxman to cure the

Indian cricket team's batting malaise. Thrashed by 10 wickets inside three days in the First Test and following on 274 runs behind in the Second, the prognosis looked terminal.

At the end of the third day, they were still 20 runs behind with V.V.S. Laxman on 109 not out. Rahul Dravid, who had swapped places with Laxman and was now batting at No.6, was 7 not out.

At the end of the fourth day, they were both still batting. They added 335 runs during the day without being parted. Laxman lived up to his Very Very Special nickname, ending the day on 275 not out. Dravid was 155 not out and neither gave a chance throughout the day.

The same two players batting all day in a Test match doesn't happen very often. (Geoff Marsh and Mark Taylor did it against England at Nottingham in 1989). It must be incredibly dispiriting still to be bowling at the same two batsmen at six o'clock in the evening that you started bowling to at eleven o'clock in the morning.

Shane Warne was hit for 152 runs off his 34 overs in the innings and only got one wicket. Kasprowich toiled away for 35 over for 139 runs without reward. McGrath and Gillespie, who had bowled so successfully in the First Test, also had three figures in the 'runs against' column.

V.V.S. Laxman was finally out for 281 early on the fifth day, going for quick runs. *Wisden* ranks it among the Top Ten Test innings of all time. Not only had it rescued his team from certain defeat, the rate that he had scored his runs allowed Ganguly to declare on the last day and give India an outside chance of victory.

The Australians were set 383 to win or try and survive for seventy-five overs. A draw looked strong favourite as Hayden and Slater put on 74 in twenty-three overs. But once Harbhajan Singh got Slater out, wickets began to fall. Tendulkar took 3 for 31 with his leg spinners and Harbhajan finished with 6 wickets, including Gilchrist for a king pair.

Australia were all out in the 69th over and their winning sequence had come to an end in spectacular fashion. Only three sides have won Test matches after being asked to follow on, one each century, and they were all against Australia. England famously did it at Headingley in 1981 and before that you have to go back to 1894 when England won in Sydney.

The three match series was now in the balance at one game all and the teams moved on to Chennai. Steve Waugh won the toss for the third time and chose to bat first. That Australia managed to score 391 was mainly due to a belligerent double century from Matthew Hayden which include fifteen fours and six sixes. Steve Waugh became only the sixth batsman in Test cricket to be given out 'handled ball'[9] when a ball from Harbhajan Singh hit his pads and spun back towards the stumps. Harbhajan was denied a wicket this time but took seven others in the innings.

India replied with 501, thanks mainly to an outstanding century from Tendulkar. Laxman and Dravid both contributed again with half centuries. Australia's second innings started solidly but collapsed again to Harbhajan Singh. He took 8 for 84 in under 42 overs, giving him fifteen wickets in the match.

India only needed 155 to win and, when they reached 100 with just 2 wickets down, it looked like a formality. But this extraordinary series had yet another twist in store. Jason Gillespie removed Tendulkar caught at second slip by Mark Waugh. Ganguly and Dravid followed in the next three overs. While V.V.S. was still there, India were safe but immediately after tea Laxman was

9 Russell Endean, Andrew Hilditch, Mohsin Khan, Desmond Haynes, and Graham Gooch were the others. Michael Vaughan was also dismissed against India this way later in the same year as Waugh.

brilliantly caught by Mark Waugh for 66, this time at mid-wicket. Bahutule, a leg spinner on début, was out immediately and India still needed 20 to win with 7 wickets down.

Débutant wicket-keeper Sameer Dighe stood firm with Zaheer Khan, but McGrath was brought back for one last effort. He dismissed Khan with yet another catch from Mark Waugh. By now only 4 runs were needed and Harbhajan had the honour of hitting the winning run.

V.V.S. Laxman had played one of the all time great Test innings and followed it up with two dashing fifties to help steer India home in the deciding Test. He would have reasonably expected to win the Man of the Series award. Instead it went to Harbhajan Singh. Twenty years old and with only a handful of Tests behind him, Harbhajan had taken 32 wickets in the series. Tendulkar was the next most successful Indian bowler with 3 wickets. Only George Lohmann, Richard Hadlee and the great Sydney Barnes have taken more wickets in a three match series. Harbhajan was to go on and be a thorn in the side of the Australians for the next decade.

Although he had made his Test début in 1996, V.V.S. Laxman had not been certain of his place in the Indian side before this series. A truly gifted player equally assured on either side of the wicket, Laxman has been an integral part of the formidable Indian batting line up for over a decade now. He has played over one hundred Tests and, if his average of a little under 50 stops him from being labelled 'great', there are few batsmen in the world who are more enjoyable to watch, unless you happen to be an Australian bowler.

Like D.E.V. Padgett and I.V.A. Richards before him, I still always look for V.V.S. Laxman's score first. It's only a mild affliction. It doesn't do anyone any harm. It's good to have obsessions as long as they don't completely take over your life or do damage to other people. It's really just about having an emotional connection with things. I've managed to convince myself that this is true and that's all that really matters!

5. England tour of South Africa, 1913/14

It is always difficult to judge these things but S.F. Barnes has a strong claim to be the greatest bowler who ever lived. His long career was coming to an end when Sir Don Bradman started playing and so the cricket world was denied the intriguing confrontation of Barnes bowling to Bradman.

Sir Jack Hobbs, whose 197 first-class centuries and sheer brilliance makes him a strong contender to Bradman as the best batsman who ever lived, played at the same time as Barnes. Hobbs was not given to hyperbole and said simply that Sydney Barnes "was the greatest bowler ever". C.L.R. James, not known for being loose with his praise, described him as "the greatest of all bowlers".

The tour that set the seal on his greatness was the one to South Africa in 1913/14. It is not possible to fully appreciate his achievements on that tour without first looking at how he came to be opening the bowling for England in South Africa at the ripe old age of forty.

Barnes's cricket career up to that point had been somewhat idiosyncratic. He was first picked for England in 1901 when he was selected to go to Australia after a season playing for Burnley in the Lancashire League. Not exactly the traditional route into the England team, even in those days. A century later, Jimmy Anderson followed in his footsteps. He had not played any first-class cricket when he was picked for England in a One-day International. He had, however, played for Burnley.

Sydney Barnes had two people to thank for being on the boat to Australia. One was Archie MacLaren, the Lancashire captain and the other was Lord Hawke, Yorkshire's captain for twenty-eight years and president for forty years. An aspiring Tyke demigod, Lord Hawke insisted that all players who represented the county should be born in Yorkshire although he himself was born in Lincolnshire. An Eton and Cambridge education obviously provides you with a philosophical sophistication that enables you to accept apparent inconsistencies in life.

MacLaren was the England captain at the time and it was the captain's job to select a team to go to Australia.[10] He naturally wanted to take Wilfred Rhodes and George Hirst, two of the best bowlers in England. Unfortunately for him, they both played for Yorkshire and Lord Hawke vetoed their selection for England. He wanted them 'fresh' to play for Yorkshire the following season and evidently felt that a tour to Australia would tire them out. Yorkshire first, England second was his view. There are still a number of sympathisers to this approach in the county today.

Rhodes and Hirst had just helped bowl Yorkshire to the Championship title. There was intense rivalry between Lancashire and Yorkshire in general and MacLaren and Hawke in particular. Lord Hawke dominated Yorkshire cricket at the time, and he wasn't about to help out his Lancastrian rival, even if it was in England's cause. MacLaren needed to look elsewhere for a cutting edge to his bowling attack to take on the Australians.

News of the bowling exploits of Sydney Barnes in the Lancashire League had reached the ears of Archie MacLaren and he invited him to play for Lancashire in the last championship match of the season. Barnes bowled superbly, taking 6 for 70 in

10 After 1901/02, the MCC took over the organisation of tours and selection of teams.

the first innings. This was enough to convince MacLaren to take him to Australia.

Had it not been for the mutual antipathy between Lord Hawke and Archie MacLaren, who fought their own personal wars of the roses over many years, Barnes would never have gone to Australia in 1901 and may never have even played Test cricket. They were to have an influence on Barnes's cricketing career for the rest of the decade.

When talking about S.F. Barnes, the word 'uncompromising' is never far away. In a time when people were supposed to know their place, he refused to bow to the expectations of others. Bowling was his profession and he was proud of it. He knew the value of what he did and if others did not have the same valuation then he would never concede any ground. He would simply take his skills elsewhere.

Born in Staffordshire, Barnes made his first-class début for Warwickshire in 1895 at the age of twenty-two. It was Warwickshire's inaugural year as a first-class county and they were on the look out for new talent. Barnes didn't make the grade and was deemed surplus to requirements. As decisions go, this must rank alongside Decca Records choosing not to sign the Beatles. (Decca said that "guitar groups are on the way out" and "the Beatles have no future in show business". Instead they signed The Tremeloes who had auditioned on the same day.)

So what kind of bowler was S.F. Barnes? Was he fast or slow? Did he seam it or spin it? The truth is that he was all of these things, and more. He is not easy to categorise. A spin bowler who opened the bowling. A fast medium bowler who could be singularly quick. C.B. Fry, who captained him in Test matches said of him: "In the matter of pace he may be regarded as a fast or a fast medium bowler. He certainly bowled faster some days than others; and on his fastest day was certainly distinctly fast"

Barnes was over six feet tall. Lean and gaunt, he was the perfect build for a bowler. When he first started playing cricket, he was an out and out fast bowler. He soon realised that speed alone was not sufficient. He reduced his pace, introduced a number of variations into his bowling and in effect became a 'fast medium spinner'. He applied 'swerve' using fingers on the ball rather than wrist action. He also developed fast off breaks and leg breaks which gave him movement off the pitch and through the air. When allied with his accuracy and ability to generate pace off the pitch, he was at times unplayable. A famous Barnes story is of two tailenders continually playing and missing against him. "They're not playing well enough to get out" he was heard to say.

Although Warwickshire didn't want Sydney Barnes, Rishton in the Lancashire League certainly did and immediately offered him a contract. Barnes was paid twice as much playing one day a week for Rishton than all week, every week in a whole season of County Championship 'grind' for Warwickshire. One can imagine that this state of affairs would have very much appealed to him.

Barnes repaid Rishton by taking 411 wickets in five years at an average of just over 9 runs each. In 1900 he moved to Burnley, one of the richest clubs in the Lancashire League. Barnes took 111 wickets at an average of 9.22 in his first season. The following year, he claimed 114 wickets at 8.11. Little wonder that Archie MacLaren was interested in getting him to play for Lancashire and England.

League cricket in the north had been established in the latter part of the 19th century. Whereas county cricket tended to be arranged to reflect the requirements of the 'gentleman amateurs', league cricket was organised around the needs of the working class. After labouring all week in the mills and factories, the workers would support their local team at the weekend. Admission prices were low, travel to the grounds was easy and the standard of cricket was high.

It's fair to say that Sydney Barnes was more at home in the relative meritocracy of league cricket. If you were good enough you would play, and be rewarded accordingly. County cricket, on the other hand, was run by, and on behalf of, the 'gentlemen amateurs'. They were not natural bedfellows for S.F. Barnes.

Batsmen were his natural prey and he was a predator supreme. Neville Cardus noted that "a chill wind of antagonism blew from him on the sunniest day." Cricket was not 'fun' it was his profession. Many years later, Barnes was playing in a charity match. Barnes was in his fifties and Learie Constantine was struggling with his batting. Cec Parkin, Barnes' captain, asked him to chuck a few up so that the crowd could see Learie Constantine hit one or two. Barnes threw down the ball, collected his sweater and refused to bowl again in the match. "I have a reputation as well as Constantine" was his retort.

Lancashire had made attempts to persuade Barnes to play for the county on a number of occasions over the years. A.N. Hornby, the Lancashire captain before Archie MacLaren, wanted to have a look at him so gave Barnes a late entry into a League XI for a friendly game at Old Trafford. Barnes turned him down on the grounds that as he wasn't originally selected he wouldn't play just to make up the numbers.

On another occasion, Barnes agreed to turn out in a trial match but, when he discovered that he was in the second team, he declined to play. Apart from his natural cussedness, the crux of the issue was that Barnes could get paid more for doing less if he played league cricket. Unless the terms were exactly to his liking, he had no reason to submit himself to the rigours of county cricket. When Hornby was told what Barnes was being paid for his performances in the Lancashire League, he supposedly replied that he could get three professionals for the same amount. One can only imagine what the response of Barnes would have been had he heard him say this!

Where Hornby had failed, MacLaren succeeded. Not only did he persuade the Lancashire committee to offer Barnes a contract, he also managed to get Barnes to accept it. On his return from Australia in 1902, Sydney Barnes was due to play his first full season in county cricket.

Archie MacLaren had a number of run-ins both with the Lancashire hierarchy and the Lords authorities. He was very much his own man, as he showed by taking Sydney Barnes to Australia. The southern-based media at the time had been shocked at the selection of Barnes and some openly questioned MacLaren's sanity. MacLaren and Barnes had their differences but maintained a grudging respect for each other. It probably did not extend beyond the cricket field. On the trip to Australia, the ship carrying the England touring party ran into severe storms. Trying to comfort his less experienced colleagues, MacLaren said: "If we do go down, at least that bugger Barnes will go down with us!"

Barnes proved to be a great success in Australia. After doing well in the state games, he was selected for his first Test in Sydney on 13th December 1901. England batted first and MacLaren scored a century. Barnes contributed to the total of 464 with 26 not out. When Australia batted, Barnes soon had his first Test victim. He caught and bowled Victor Trumper, Australia's premier batsman and one of the best players of all time. Many people, including some Australians, regard him as having been a better batsman than Bradman. Perhaps that's why Barnes got Trumper out so often? He was usually good enough to get a touch.

Barnes bowled virtually unchanged for the entire innings taking 5 for 65 off 35.1 overs and Australia were all out for 168. When they followed on they were bowled out for 172. Barnes, probably exhausted from his first innings effort, only got one of the wickets. Braund and Blythe got the rest. Against the odds and most people's expectations, England had beaten a very strong Australian side and Barnes had established himself as a Test bowler.

The Second Test in Melbourne was another step along the way to making Sydney Barnes the world's greatest bowler. Australia were bowled out in the first innings for 112 with Barnes taking 6 for 42. For England however, this was as good as it was going to get. They, in turn, were bundled out for 61 and although Barnes helped to reduce Australia to 48 for 5 in their second innings, they recovered to score a total of 353.

In Australia's second innings, Barnes bowled 64 overs in the heat and humidity of Melbourne, taking 7 for 121. It was a monumental effort but all in vain. England were bowled out for 175 and they lost the match. Barnes's exertions on the hard Australian pitches took their toll. He developed knee problems and, although MacLaren took a risk and picked him for the third Test, he was only able to bowl seven overs. Barnes didn't play again on the tour and England lost the three remaining Test matches.

The Australian team came back on the same boat as the England players in order to take part in the return Ashes series. Barnes was recovering from his knee injury so was not considered for the first two Tests. It mattered little as England were able to put out what is considered to be one of their finest XIs ever. All the players who didn't tour Australia were now available for selection.

This was the so called Golden Age of cricket and the names resonate even now. Archie MacLaren was captain again. C.B. Fry and Ranjitsinhji made themselves available. F.S. Jackson and

Gilbert Jessop certainly didn't weaken the side. Nor did Tyldesley, Lockwood and Braund. Dick Lilley was the keeper and Lord Hawke very graciously allowed Rhodes and Hirst to appear. S.F. Barnes, the greatest bowler in the world, may have struggled to get in the team!

The Australians also had a strong side and were fresh from a 4 – 1 series win at home. They also had a secret weapon. Lord Hawke was now Chairman of the England selectors and Archie MacLaren was still England's captain.

Things started well for England. They had much the better of the First Test match at Edgbaston. Only the weather saved Australia from defeat. Heavy rain meant that only two hours play was possible in the Second Test at Lords. The teams then moved on to Sheffield for the first and only Test match to be held at Bramhall Lane.

Lockwood was not available and Barnes seemed the logical choice to replace him. He had recovered from his knee problems and was bowling well for Lancashire. The England selectors, aka Lord Hawke, had other ideas. They chose Schofield Haigh, a spinner from Yorkshire.

On the morning of the match, MacLaren looked at the conditions and immediately cabled Barnes to get over to Sheffield as soon as possible. He arrived five minutes after play had started and replaced Haigh on the field. This came as a complete surprise to Lord Hawke and the other selectors. A Lancashire player replacing a Yorkshire player, even if it was Sydney Barnes, didn't go down too well either with the thousands of Yorkshiremen gathered to watch the first ever Test match in Sheffield.

As soon as Barnes was allowed to bowl, MacLaren brought him on. Heckled by the Yorkshire crowd, Barnes responded by taking four quick wickets and Australia were in trouble at 73 for 5. They recovered somewhat but Barnes came back to get two more wickets and finish with 6 for 49. This was his home début and the figures will remain forevermore as the best Test bowling figures at Bramhall Lane.

England did not bat well and collapsed for 145, some 50 runs short of a first innings lead. When Australia batted again, Barnes got Joe Darling out for a duck for the second time in the match, but Victor Trumper and Clem Hill scored heavily and England were left a target of 339 to win.

By the time England started their second innings, the smoke from the factories that surrounded Bramhall Lane made visibility very difficult and conditions were not conducive to being outside let alone playing cricket. England were all out for 195 with only MacLaren and Jessop making a significant contribution.

The next match was at Old Trafford and Lord Hawke got his revenge, Barnes was dropped. Technically of course, he hadn't been picked in the first place, so Hawke probably maintained that he wasn't being dropped, just not selected.

This was to be one of the most famous Test matches ever, and inextricably linked with Fred Tate, the man who effectively replaced Sydney Barnes. Victor Trumper scored a century before lunch and Australia reached a total of 299. England in reply scored 262 with F.S. Jackson scoring 128. Australia were then skittled out for 86, but early in the innings Fred Tate dropped Darling, who top scored with 37, on the square leg boundary.

England only needed 124 to win but subsided to the bowling of Trumble. Tate was clean bowled with only 4 needed. Australia had won "Fred Tate's match", and the Ashes, by 3 runs. It seems certain that Barnes would have made a difference had he been playing. It might be a bit of a stretch to say that Trumper was his 'rabbit' (come up with your own Sun headline employing the word 'Thumper!') but Barnes did get him out thirteen times in twenty Tests. In addition, he had dismissed all the top Australian batsmen cheaply in their previous encounters.

It was hard on Tate who was a decent county bowler – he had had an outstanding season for Sussex on the wet wickets of 1902, taking 153 wickets for them. This proved to be his one and only Test match but he did contribute to England's cause by fathering a talented son. Maurice Tate took 155 wickets in thirty-nine Tests for England – ironically in a style not dissimilar to Sydney Barnes, and was a good enough batsman to score a Test century.

Barnes wasn't selected for the last match at the Oval either. Gilbert Jessop, who had also been inexplicably dropped for the Old Trafford Test, was recalled and scored one of the fastest ever Test centuries off only 76 balls. He had gone in at 48 for 5 with England needing 263 to win. Hirst and Rhodes with the apocryphal "we'll get 'em in singles" got the 15 runs needed in a last wicket partnership.

Like a fleeting, brilliant meteor in the sky, it looked like the Test career of Sydney Barnes was over. A victim of the small-minded squabbles between MacLaren and Hawke and his own stubborn nature. After a successful second season with Lancashire, when he took 131 wickets at an average of seventeen runs each, Barnes seemingly engineered his own dismissal. He had demanded an improvement on the one pound a week that the county was prepared to pay him in the winter. Not an unreasonable request you would think from a player who had bowled more overs and taken more wickets than any of his team-mates.

Nevertheless, it was not one that the gentlemen of the Lancashire committee felt they could accede to. Barnes turned up for a match towards the end of the season and was told that his services were no longer required. He was summarily sent home. That showed him who was in charge!

Barnes probably wasn't too concerned. He signed for Church in the Lancashire League where he would be paid twice as much for half the work. Predictably, he was not considered for the tour to Australia in the winter of 1903. At the age of thirty, that looked like the end of his first-class career. He had played a couple of seasons of county cricket and four Test matches. The normal scenario would be a few more years playing in the league and then retire to maybe run a post office or open a pub.

However, that was not the Barnes way of doing things. Although he performed well for Church they did not win the league as they had expected. After two seasons, he was offered a reduced contract. Barnes being Barnes would not accept that and he moved back to the county of his birth.

He joined Porthill Park and for the next nine years played in the lesser known North Staffordshire League. During this time he was to appear in another twenty-three Test matches and establish himself as the preeminent bowler of his era and arguably the greatest bowler of all time. Not many cricketers performing in the North Staffs League would be on the national selectors' radar, especially a player who had ruffled a few feathers as Barnes had done. Also, without Barnes, England had won the series in Australia in 1903/04 (Lord Hawke had allowed Rhodes and Hirst to go this time). When the Australians returned in 1905, England retained the Ashes, winning two games and drawing the others. In addition, although England lost the series in South Africa in the winter of 1905/06, they gained revenge at home the following year. Again, Barnes had not been considered for selection in any of the Tests.

So how did Sydney Barnes get back in the England squad that sailed to Australia at the end of 1907? The main reason was the surfeit of first-class cricket played at this time and the sheer length of time that a tour to Australia took a player away from his home and family, and, in the case of some amateurs, their business interests. A number of the top players were not available to tour. Others were in decline and no longer the force they used to be.

Barnes, on the other hand, even at the age of thirty five was relatively fresh. He benefited from having played less cricket over the years and was still approaching his prime. He was far too good for the batsmen in the North Staffordshire League. In 1907, he took 112 wickets at an average of 3.91. It must have been a double-edged experience for any batsman playing against Porthill Park at the time. They didn't score any runs but at least they could say that they had faced the great S.F. Barnes!

He also started playing for Staffordshire and continued to do so until 1935, taking 1,441 wickets at an average of just over 8 runs each. Barnes took all ten wickets at the cost of only 26 runs against a reasonably strong Yorkshire Second XI in the 1907 season. If Lord Hawke didn't see it, he would certainly have heard about it. Maybe it was that performance that got Barnes on the boat to Australia?

An under-strength and inexperienced England team took on a strong Australian side very keen to regain the Ashes in 1907. England lost the First Test by two wickets and then Barnes, the all-rounder, came to the fore in the next Test at Melbourne. He took yet another 'fifer' (5 for 72 off 27 overs) and, batting at No. 9, featured in a last wicket stand of 40, scoring 38 not out and hitting the winning run. The series was level.

However, Australia won the next two matches thus winning back the Ashes. There were modest contributions from Barnes; always economical but without the spectacular success he was used to. Normal service for Barnes was resumed in the last Test at Sydney. He destroyed the Australian batting with 7 for 60 off twenty-two overs. England scored 281 and established a first innings lead of 144.

Even though the series had already been won, the Australians did not give up. Victor Trumper was dropped off Barnes when only 1 and then made England pay by going on to score a brilliant 166. Barnes, probably tired after bowling more overs than anyone else on tour and maybe sulking about the dropped chance, only got one wicket and England were set 279 to win. A last wicket stand between Barnes and Crawford of 31 took them to within 50 runs of victory but there was to be no repeat of the Second Test heroics.

Although England had lost the series by four Tests to one, Barnes had done well again. He had taken 24 wickets and always been shown respect by the Australian batsmen. Charlie Marcartney, the Australian batting at the other end, described a ball that Barnes bowled to Victor Trumper: "The ball was fast on the leg stump but just before it pitched, it swung suddenly to the off. Then it pitched, broke back, and took Vic's leg stump. It was the sort of ball a man might see if he was dreaming or drunk."

It would not have been unreasonable for Barnes to expect to be in the side to face Australia in the First Test at Edgbaston in the summer of 1909. Lord Hawke, in his wisdom, thought otherwise.

He didn't pick Barnes but he did give in to media pressure, which played its part a hundred years ago as it does today, and recalled Archie MacLaren to the team as captain. For any number of reasons, this was an extraordinary decision. They manifestly did not get on and their mutual enmity was not going to help win back the Ashes. On top of that MacLaren, at the age of thirty-eight, was well past his best. In his prime he was a supreme, commanding batsman. In 1895 he scored 424 for Lancashire at Taunton against Somerset which remained the highest first-class score for the next thirty years.

By the time the Australians arrived in 1909, he was no longer captain of Lancashire and hadn't played Test cricket for a few years.

Allen Synge, in his book *Sins of Omission*, which describes mistakes made by England selectors over the years, likens Hawke and MacLaren to two cantankerous and argumentative characters in an over-long Samuel Becket play who are eternally linked in misfortune for England.

Beckett, the only Nobel Prize winner ever to appear in *Wisden*, would surely have approved of the analogy. I don't think the use of the expression "over-long" is a deliberate attempt at a pun. Even Steve Harmison would be hard pushed to bowl an over long enough to contain a Beckett play.

If MacLaren had wanted Barnes in his team, he was not successful in getting him. To the surprise of the public, players and press, Barnes was not selected for the first two games. If the Australians were equally puzzled by his omission they were certainly not unhappy. As it turned out, England managed to win the first Test but the selectors contrived to make five changes for the next game, only two enforced. England went into the Second Test at Lords without a fast bowler and lost by 9 wickets.

Finally, Barnes was recalled for the Third Test at Headingley. He took 1 for 37 off twenty-five overs in the first innings and then 6 for 63 off thirty-five overs in the second. Despite his efforts, England lost the match. Barnes got another 'fifer' (5 for 56) in the drawn Test at Old Trafford. No doubt the Lancashire committee enjoyed watching his performance. The Oval Test was also a draw and Australia had retained the Ashes.

Once again, the MacLaren/Hawke/Barnes triumvirate had failed. 1909 saw the end of MacLaren's fine Test career. Lord Hawke was finally relieved of his duties as a national selector but Barnes was named as one of *Wisden's* 'Five Cricketers of the Year'.

It seems that at last, Sydney Barnes had established himself as an England regular. Even though he went back to playing for Porthill Park and Staffordshire, he was selected to go to Australia in October 1911. He had taken part in four series against the Australians and had been on the losing side each time. He had always performed well himself but was he an unlucky omen for the England team? The signs were not good at the start of his fifth attempt to win the Ashes.

First of all, C.B. Fry was asked to lead the side but could not spare the time. So Plum Warner was invited to take on the England captaincy. He in turn was taken ill early on the tour and was unable to play in any of the Test matches. The widely held view at the time was that it would be the end of civilisation as we know it if a professional captained England.[11] There were only two other amateurs in the touring party – Douglas and Foster – so one of them had to be captain.

The job fell to J.W.H.T. Douglas, the captain of Essex, playing in his first ever Test series. His nickname was 'Johnnie Won't Hit Today' which I suppose makes a change from 'Douglasy' or whatever similar sobriquet he would be given if he was playing now. He was a gentleman all-rounder and a good county player. How he got on with Sydney Barnes was going to be a key factor in determining the success of the tour.

The First Test was at Sydney and the portents were not good. Johnnie Douglas decided to open the bowling himself, along with fellow amateur Frank Foster. Barnes's response was quite restrained

---

11 It was another forty years before the cricket authorities felt it was safe to appoint a professional as captain. Len Hutton had that honour in 1952. He won each of his first five Test series as captain. The distinction between amateur and professional was finally abolished in 1962. For some people, the world has never been the same since.

in the circumstances. "That's all very well Mr Douglas, but what am I 'ere for?" was his observation. He could not comprehend how someone other than himself could open the bowling and wasn't afraid to air his views. His fellow professionals were equally bemused and one can imagine that the Australian opening batsmen had to pinch themselves when they heard the news.

Predictably, the Australians made hay in the sunshine, scoring 447 including a century from Victor Trumper. Barnes bowled steadily when he eventually came on but the damage had been done. England went on to lose the match by 146 runs.

Barnes and England were on course for another series defeat. Something had to be done. There was an England team meeting to discuss what had gone wrong. To Douglas's credit he, in modern parlance, 'took on board the feedback'. First of all, Wilfred Rhodes completed his journey up the batting order from England's No.11 to opening batsman and began his eminently successful partnership with Jack Hobbs. Secondly, it was agreed that it might be a good idea if Sydney Barnes opened the bowling.

There was an immediate reward in the Second Test at Melbourne when Barnes produced one of the most incisive and dramatic spells of bowling seen in Test cricket. Here is Plum Warner's description of the start of the match:

"Hill won the toss.......there was a beautiful wicket ..... Foster opened the attack and Barnes bowled from the railway end. One heard on all sides that Australia would make a big score. Foster bowls a maiden to Kelleway, then Barnes takes the ball. Tall, upright, broad and fit looking, he is full of life as he runs up to the wicket. A few steps, then a couple of strides with both feet off the ground together, and the ball is delivered with concentration and marked energy."

The first ball from Barnes bowled Bardsley off his pads. Next ball, the captain, Clem Hill took a single. This was to be the only run off Barnes for an hour. After another maiden, Kelleway missed an inswinger from Barnes and was LBW. Australia were 5 for 2. The final ball from Barnes next over pitched on Hill's leg stump and hit the top off. The home side were 8 for 3. This is how Hill describes his experience of facing Barnes in that innings:

> "I was in first wicket down, after Bardsley had gone for 0. I got four, probably from Foster ... I wanted to get away from Barnes. I played three different balls. Three balls to play in a split second – a straight 'un, an in swinger and a break back! Then along came one which was straight half way, not more than medium pace. (Then) It swerved to my legs, perfect for tickling round the corner for a single. But the ruddy thing (again) broke across after pitching, quick off the ground and took my off stump!"

Trumper had been put down the order to save him from the new ball. He joined Armstrong who drove Foster for three. In the next over from Barnes, Armstrong nicked his first ball and was caught behind. Australia were 11 for 4 and Barnes had four wickets for one run!

Play resumed after a short break for rain and Barnes did not seem himself. A full toss went for four byes. At the end of the over Barnes had to leave the field. He had been unwell all week and nearly did not play. After lunch, Foster bowled Trumper with the total on 33 and Barnes was back on the field. Minnett, who had scored a fine 90 in the First Test, came in and immediately nicked Barnes to third slip and was dropped. After scoring two runs, he skied Barnes to Jack Hobbs at cover and Australia had collapsed to 38 for 6.

Barnes, who came off his sickbed to play, had the extraordinary figures of 11 overs, 7 maidens, 5 wickets for 6 runs. He didn't get any more wickets in the innings and finished with 5 for 44 off twenty-three overs. He nearly had the last wicket of Whitty. All the players, including Whitty himself, thought that he had been clean bowled. As they trooped off the field, Bob Crockett,[12] the umpire at square leg, insisted that the ball had come off the wicket-keeper's pads and called them all back. Whitty was given not out and the last pair added another 35 runs enabling Australia to reach a total of 184, veritable riches after being 38 runs for 6 wickets down.

An incident occurred during Australia's innings that illustrates the testy side of Barnes's character but also his mental strength. At 125 for 8, he had been brought back to try and finish off the innings. He was meticulous in his field placing – and it was always him that set his field not the captain. He was taking rather longer than usual to get the field just how he wanted it and some of the crowd started barracking and telling him "to get on with it" and other such terms of encouragement.

Barnes resented this, threw down the ball, folded his arms and refused to bowl until the noise stopped. He was a professional, going about his business. It didn't matter to him that he was in the middle of a Test match surrounded by thousands of Australians. He was not prepared to carry on if some of the Aussie hoi polloi were going to jeer at him. Luckily for him, the Melbourne members did not approve of the barracking and cheered his act of defiance.

An Australian critic wrote the next day:

"It was a most unwarranted display against a man who had bowled magnificently. It evidenced, too, a most partisan spirit. It was confined

---

12 Crockett was the umpire who no balled Jack Marsh, the Aborigine fast bowler, nineteen times in a state match. The crowd jeered every time he called 'no ball', but he persisted until Marsh was taken off.

to a hostile section in the shilling stand and such unfair treatment undoubtedly interfered with Barnes's bowling. In his next over there was a similar outbreak by the hoodlums, but the occupants of the members' reserve cheered him and the noisy element was quickly quelled by the counter demonstration."

"During the tea interval, the demonstration against Barnes was universally condemned and it was suggested that the Victorian authorities should at once follow the example of the New South Wales Association and announce that they would prosecute offenders for unruly or riotous behaviour."

Nice to see Australian press support for an England player!

Barnes had made his point to the crowd and, more importantly, he had made his point to the Australian batsmen. Hearne hit a century and Rhodes scored 61 when England batted and they established a first innings lead of 81. Foster got 6 for 91 in Australia's second innings and there were another 3 wickets for Barnes. England only needed 219, which they reached comfortably. They lost only 2 wickets. Jack Hobbs completing the first of his twelve centuries against Australia.

England had achieved a remarkable victory against all expectations. Barnes's opening spell when he had destroyed the Australian top order had inflicted a major psychological blow. In the next Test at Adelaide, England went 2 – 1 up, with Barnes taking another 8 wickets and Hobbs getting his highest ever Test score of 187.

Then it was back to Melbourne again. Australia were put in by Douglas and bowled out for 191 on the first day with Barnes taking 5 for 74. England then amassed 589 with a record opening partnership from Hobbs and Rhodes of 323. Johnnie Douglas showed that he too could bowl a bit by taking 5 wickets and Australia were bowled out a second time for 173. The Ashes had come home! England went on to win the last Test too and Barnes finished the series with 34 wickets. Not bad for a thirty-eight-year-old North Staffordshire League player.

The next opportunity that Barnes had to demonstrate his bowling prowess on the international stage was the Triangular Tournament in the summer of 1912. South Africa were now considered strong enough to compete with England and Australia. The ICC (the Imperial Cricket Council as it was known as then) decided to hold an international championship every four years.

The Tournament did not go well and was not repeated. First of all, the weather that summer was very poor and three of the nine Test matches had to be abandoned due to rain. Secondly, as the *Daily Telegraph* pointed out at the time: "Nine Tests provide a surfeit of cricket, and contests between Australia and South Africa are not a great attraction to the British public." Finally, although England were able to field a very capable side, the other two countries were under strength.

South Africa were not the force they had been a few years earlier when they had beaten England. They still had two world class batsman in A.D. Nourse and Herbie Taylor but many of their teammates struggled in the English conditions. Australia were not able to field their best side. In a forerunner to the Packer crisis of the late 1970s, the Australian players were in dispute with the Australian Cricket Board. Six of their top players, including Clem Hill and Victor Trumper, didn't make the trip.

England, led by C.B. Fry, won the Tournament winning four Tests and drawing the other two. Barnes continued where he had left off in Australia. He took an incredible 34 wickets in three games against South Africa. Test matches in England at the time were played over three days only. This fact, combined with the poor weather, meant that England's first two games with Australia were draws. In the deciding match against Australia at the Oval, Barnes took 5 for 30 in the first innings off twenty-seven overs to once again blow away the Australian batsmen. This was to be a 'timeless Test' to ensure a result but England wrapped up victory on the fourth day.

Aside from the exploits of Sydney Barnes, the most notable incident of the series was Australia's Jimmy Matthews taking two hat tricks in the same Test match. He got one in each innings of the opening match against South Africa. This is the only time that a bowler has taken two hat tricks in the same match in Test history, a record that seems likely to remain unbroken. Both hat tricks were taken on the same day after South Africa followed on. Amazingly, Matthews took no other wickets in the match. Another curiosity is that the third victim in each case was débutant wicket-keeper Tommy Ward. The only 'King Pair' achieved on début in Test cricket, an unenviable record.

In *Wisden's* review of the 1912 season, Barnes was described as "the best bowler in the world." It continued "The skill with which he broke both ways while keeping a perfect length all the time, was wonderful." In those days, *Wisden* was very much part of the cricket establishment and over the years it had been reluctant to give full credit to Barnes for his achievements. Barnes's stubbornness and his sense of self worth shine through in his every confrontation. He was the Keir Hardie of cricket, sixty years ahead of his time in his rejection of the class system that dominated the English cricket world. This naturally did not go down well with the cricket authorities. Now though, *Wisden* had been finally won over.

Barnes had achieved great things and all on his own terms. 140 Test wickets at an average of just under 18. A major contribution to winning the Ashes back for England. Player of the Tournament in the first 'world championship'. There was one performance left which would confirm his divine status. The tour to South Africa in the winter of 1913/14.

With only three countries playing Test cricket, sometimes there were no Test matches during a summer and that was the case in 1913. So Barnes went back to playing for Porthill Park and Staffordshire. He did however play regularly, and with great success, in the Gentlemen v Players games. These were usually in front of full houses at Lords or the Oval and deemed by Barnes to be a fitting stage for his talents. These games may seem anachronistic nowadays but they did provide Barnes with an opportunity to play first-class cricket and he probably enjoyed putting one over the amateur gentlemen.

He reminded the cricket upper echelons of his existence by turning out for the Players XI in July that year. After taking 2 for 67 in twenty-five overs in the Gentlemen's first innings, he took 7 for 38 in the second to help the Players to victory. That was Barnes' only first-class game that year until September but it certainly made sure that he was not forgotten.

During September, Barnes warmed up for the tour to South Africa by playing in some representative first-class games including the Rest of England against a combined Kent and Yorkshire XI at the Oval. He bowled his team to victory with 7 for 20 in the second innings. He had taken 35 wickets in the four first-class games he played that year and had booked his place on the boat to South Africa.

In the last Test series before the First World War – there was to be no more international cricket until 1920 – Sydney Barnes, at the age of forty, set records that have still not been matched today. He did it in his own relentless, dominating style and the tour ended with a classic Barnes dénouement.

He had been to South Africa once before when he coached and played for Claremont Cricket Club in Cape Town in the winter of 1898/99. This experience and the good form that he had been in towards the end of the summer stood him in good stead at the start of the tour. He got 36 wickets in four warm up matches and was primed for the First Test at Durban.

Barnes took 5 for 57 in South Africa's first innings with only Herbie Taylor able to play him with any confidence. Taylor scored 109 out of a final total of 182 and was the last man to be dismissed. This was the start of an epic battle between the best bowler in the world and one of the best batsmen in the world. Barnes got him cheaply in the second innings as well as four other victims and England had won the first Test.

Many years later, Barnes was asked which batsman he had found most difficult to bowl to. He replied "Victor Trumper". When asked if there was anyone else, he retorted "No one else ever troubled me." This gives a clue to the confidence, some might say arrogance, that Barnes had. He could have given Herbie Taylor a mention. In a series totally dominated by Barnes, Taylor scored over 500 runs and was the only batsman that ever looked comfortable against him.

The second and third Tests were both played at Johannesburg. Barnes produced a performance in the Second Test that is still the second best bowling figures ever achieved in Test matches: 17 wickets for 159 runs. This is what *Wisden* had to say:

> "It was Barnes's match. On no occasion was the great bowler seen to quite such advantage. He took 17 wickets – 8 for 56 and 9 for 103 – proving quite irresistible on the last morning."

Wilfred Rhodes and Phil Mead scored centuries and England won by an innings and 12 runs. The Third Test was closer. South Africa were set 396 to win in the last innings and when Taylor and Zulch made 153 for the first wicket, it looked like they might do it. Barnes was made to struggle for just about the first time on the tour. After the first wicket fell, South Africa collapsed and England eventually won by 91 runs, Barnes took 5 for 102. Together with his 3 wickets from the first innings, Barnes now had 35 wickets from only three Tests.

In the tour games immediately after the Third Test, Barnes continued to take wickets. His final total of first-class wickets for the tour was 104 from just twelve games. In addition, he took another 21 wickets in two games not classified as first-class.

Around this time, he seemed to relax, or was tired or thought it was too easy and Herbie Taylor took full advantage. Barnes had a modest game against Transvaal and then, in the last game before the Fourth Test, the tourists took on Natal. Taylor scored 91 in the first innings and a century in the second, and England lost their only match of the tour. Barnes did get 5 for 44 in the first innings but only 2 for 70 in the second.

It was during this second innings that Barnes is alleged to have lost his cool. On the matting wickets of South Africa, Herbie Taylor was supreme. He had exquisite footwork and in Natal's second innings he was playing Barnes with ease. Taylor would recount in later years that Barnes was so exasperated that he threw down the ball and refused to bowl. "It's Taylor, Taylor, Taylor, all the time" he is reputed to have said.

Barnes later refuted these claims but, whether it was true or not, it usefully illustrates the perfectionism of the man. He could not tolerate second best in anyone, including himself. South Africa went into the Fourth Test in a positive mood. They had run England close in the previous Test. Natal had just beaten the tourists and their champion batsman had just had the better of England's premier bowler.

Barnes now proved his greatness and responded with 7 for 56 to bowl South Africa out for 170. When it was England's turn to bat, only Jack Hobbs coped with the home side's attack and for the first time in the series, South Africa had a first innings lead. Taylor scored 93 in the second innings, winning another round with Barnes but England's leading bowler had the last laugh by taking 7 for 88 to give him 14 wickets in the match. Hobbs fell just short of a century as England hung on for a draw at 154 for 5.

Barnes now had 49 wickets in the series. He already had the most number of wickets ever taken in a Test series and there was still one game to go. Having averaged over 10 wickets in each Test so far, it was reasonable to expect him to go on and set a record that would never be beaten. Immortality was within his grasp.

What Sydney Barnes did now was typical of the man and showed that he had not yet mellowed with the years. The England team arrived in Bloemfontein for the last Test. Barnes believed that the South Africans had promised him some money as a special payment for his performances. When it was not forthcoming, he was so upset that he refused to play in the Test match or again on tour.

One can imagine Johnnie Douglas, the captain, desperately trying to persuade him to play and all his entreaties falling on deaf ears. True to form, Barnes would not budge from his position. He was using the same single minded, rigorous approach to his affairs off the field that he applied to his bowling. Perhaps you can not have one without the other? It's just a shame that Barnes could not have seen his way through to make it out onto the pitch for that last Test and who knows how many wickets he would have finished up with in the series!

One hundred years on and 49 wickets is still the record for the number of wickets in a Test series. Only four other bowlers have taken more that 40 wickets in a series. Jim Laker with 46 wickets and Charlie Grimmett with 44 have come closest but both did it in five Tests. Terry Alderman (twice) and Rodney Hogg also got more than 40 wickets in a series but each took six Tests to achieve it.

A 'Barnesless' England went on to win the last Test and S.F. Barnes had played his last Test match. He did in fact have another opportunity to play Test cricket. Incredibly, he was invited to go on the tour of Australia in 1920/21 at the age of forty-seven but, as ever, laid down his own terms. He wanted to take his wife and child with him, paid for of course by the MCC. He reckoned that he would be happier if they were with him on tour and therefore he would bowl better. Needless to say, the authorities did not acquiesce to this request, even for the great S.F. Barnes, and so the last opportunity to add to his 189 Test wickets was gone.

Although he didn't play any more Test cricket after 1914, Barnes carried on playing league and Minor Counties cricket for another quarter of a century. Luckily for him, the best bowler in the world was deemed too old to be called up and sent to the trenches. He left Porthill Park somewhat acrimoniously after the Chairman had promised to 'look after' him come what may. Seemingly, Barnes did not think that the outbreak of the First World War was a good enough reason for him to break his word!

Barnes joined Saltaire in the Bradford League. He rewarded them over the next nine years with 904 wickets at an average of just over 5 runs per wicket. Extraordinary figures for anyone let alone a man in his forties. He then moved to the Central Lancashire League for seven years, playing for Casteleton Moor and later Rochdale, again averaging 100 wickets a season.

In 1931, he returned to the Lancashire League and played three seasons for Rawtenstall. He continued playing professional league cricket up to 1940 when he was contracted to play for Stone in the North Staffordshire & South Cheshire League. He began playing cricket before the Boer War started and finished during the early years of the Second World War. He was unique.

In 1929, at the age of fifty-six, he played for a Minor Counties XI against the touring South Africans. He bowled unchanged for three hours taking 8 for 41 in thirty-two overs. At lunch, Barnes had taken 2 wickets and a local enthusiast offered him £25 if he took all the remaining wickets in the innings. One of the South Africans had retired ill but when the last man came in, Barnes had taken all eight wickets to fall. He then marked a cross on the turf and instructed Jack Meyer, the Somerset amateur, to stand there. Barnes bowled and the ball duly came off the South African No.11's bat straight into and then out of Meyer's hands. Barnes glared, glowered, muttered and cursed. What he said when Meyer proceeded to clean bowl the Springbok No 10 with the first ball of his own next over was never recorded.

To celebrate the centenary of *Wisden* in 1963, Neville Cardus was asked to select 'Six Giants of the *Wisden* Century'. He chose W.G. Grace, Tom Richardson, Victor Trumper, Jack Hobbs, Don Bradman and . . . . Sydney Barnes. The Staffordshire League player, turned down by Warwickshire and rejected by Lancashire, had officially become a legend.

6. Ash Tree CC tour of Nantwich, 2007

If you have ever tried to get a cricket team out on a Sunday, or indeed any other day of the week, you will know that it is not a simple task. By comparison, Hercules had it easy when he had to clean out the Augean stables.

Cast iron guarantees on a Monday can be reduced to 'not sure I can make it' by Wednesday and then to 'I'm really sorry, something's come up' by Friday. Out of the blue visits to obscure relatives, unexpected obligations to do some DIY work, children's birthdays, grandchildren's birthdays, 'just remembered it's our wedding anniversary', 'a mate has got me a ticket for the United match' .... the list of potential excuses is endless.

Trying to organise an overseas Taverners cricket tour multiplies all these difficulties many times over. The Ash Tree had followed its successful tour of Menorca in 2000 with a slightly less successful trip to Mallorca. We had all got to Manchester Airport on time, which was an encouraging, if somewhat unexpected start. However, our punctuality was not rewarded as we soon discovered that the plane we should have been on was in Mallorca not Manchester, and that there would be a six hour delay. We were flying *First Choice* and someone observed that it was a good thing that we were not with Second Choice.

There was nothing we could do but repair to the *Yang Sing* in the centre of Manchester, enjoy a Chinese meal and hope that everyone got back in time for the delayed flight. We got the train from the airport into the city, had an excellent meal and thankfully everyone made it back in good time. Our plane had found its way to Manchester and we eventually arrived at Palma de Mallorca in the early hours of the next day.

We spent the first day 'acclimatising' and were due to play the MCC (Mallorca Cricket Club) the following day. We woke to pouring rain and when we got to the ground it was under water. The irony of flying all the way from Manchester to Mallorca to have a game of cricket rained off was not lost on us.

The opposition sportingly agreed to try and play a game the next day. If it had been our home pitch under that amount of water then we wouldn't have been able to play for a week. But this was Mallorca and we did indeed manage to play the following day. We performed poorly and were well beaten, but at least we had managed to get a game. It would have been a long way to go not to play any cricket at all.

For a few years afterwards, it was difficult to muster enthusiasm and, more significantly, commitment for another tour. When organising a tour, it is important to differentiate between 'enthusiasm' ("Yes, I'd love to go on a tour. Great idea.") and 'commitment' (Actually coming up with a deposit for the flights and hotel, six months before the tour takes place.)

After several aborted attempts, I was given the task of trying to organise a tour in 2007. When I say 'given', what I really mean is that I made the mistake of saying something during a discussion about possible tours that had been interpreted as volunteering actually to do something about it. In short, I had been lumbered.

No matter, I had always wanted to go to the West Indies on a cricket tour, maybe this was my chance? If that was too much of a stretch for the less adventurous club members, I had been on holiday to Corfu many years before and had seen a cricket pitch there. Assuming it was still in action, Corfu would be perfect and also give me an opportunity to give the "What's a Greek urn?" joke another airing. France was another possibility. Not too far. Good weather, good wine and good food. Despite the fact that the French air traffic controllers always seemed to go on strike in the summer, it was tempting.

So where was it to be? The West Indies, Corfu or France? We finally ended up going to .... Nantwich. Readers with a reasonable grasp of geography will have spotted that not only is Nantwich not abroad, it is actually less than thirty miles from our home base of Macclesfield.

I had failed to convert enthusiasm into commitment. Even a suggestion of five days in Devon had been met with a certain degree of misgiving. A trip to Nantwich was OK though. It was like a very extended away match but I still maintain that it was definitely, technically, a tour. We were travelling as a group. We were staying overnight. We planned to paint the town red on Saturday night (not in the *High Plains Drifter* sense but certainly trying to make sure we experienced everything a Saturday night in Nantwich had to offer). And we were going to play a game of cricket against Wistaston the next day. Well, it certainly beats cutting the lawn and washing the car.

The 'tour' took place in the middle of September and, although there was much mirth about a 'world cricket tour to Wistaston', at least some sort of activity involving travelling, drinking and cricket was taking place. The players rendezvoused at the *Admiral Rodney* in Prestbury. We had one late withdrawal when Tony was unexpectedly called away to Thailand. As excuses go, it was certainly more impressive than tea with the mother-in-law or tickets for a Boyzone concert.

While we waited in the *Admiral Rodney*, we took bets on who would arrive last. Every club has someone who is habitually late. The Ash Tree has two main candidates: Joe and Andrew. Joe shocked us all by strolling in well before the deadline; possibly the fact that we were meeting in a pub might have helped. Andrew however was not there on time. The driver of the minibus that we had hired was revving his engine, ready to set off. The 'quick half before we go' had become a couple of pints when Andrew eventually arrived with some bizarre story about having to catch some budgerigars that had escaped. You couldn't make it up.

The minibus finally started on its Nantwich odyssey. We got as far as Over Peover, which is about five miles away and not really on the direct route to Nantwich. The reason for the slight diversion was the *Park Gate Inn*. You could buy seven pints of Sam Smiths and still have change from a tenner. With no worries about drinking and driving, it was too good an opportunity to miss. Rum babas in Barbados, martinis in Corfu and a glass of Chablis in France have all got their place but you can't really beat a pint of Sam Smiths at £1.38.

While supping our beer, we had an enlightened and intellectual debate about the environment and carbon footprints. The talk moved on to polar bears and farting elks, and went downhill from there. As well as the incredibly cheap Sam Smiths, the food at the *Park Gate* was good too and at one point it looked like the tour wouldn't get any further than Over Peover. Only iron discipline from the tour manager ensured that the tour party got back on track.

Mark was still salivating about his Black Pudding Tower as we drove through Crewe, which to be honest is usually the best thing to do with Crewe. We arrived at a *Travel Lodge* just outside Nantwich which, as luck would have it, was next door to a pub called the *Peacock*. No expense was to be spared on this trip.

After booking in and a quick drink at the *Peacock*, we headed off in the direction of Nantwich. It's a delightful town with many fine hostelries, some of which we sampled before having a late evening meal.

Once we had eaten, we had one final port of call on our Saturday night Nantwich adventure. Our destination was *Nakatcha*, advertised as "the newest and hippest nitespot in Nantwich." Just five minutes walk and we found it. Outside the door were four bouncers dressed in their ubiquitous black. These bouncers are trained to spot troublemakers at twenty paces and they obviously knew they were on to something when they saw a group of veteran Taverners cricketers approaching.

As we entered the club, one of our party was apprehended by a bouncer and told that he couldn't go in. Was it the red stains on his jeans where some wine had been spilt during the meal? Was the faded denim shirt just a bit too passé for their establishment? Was he simply too old? No, it was the footwear that was unacceptable. During their training, these bouncers have part of their brain removed and a small microchip put in its place, which says 'NO TRAINERS ALLOWED'.

Nantwich farmers wearing wellington boots were allowed in. Fourteen-year-old girls in flip flops were OK but very expensive, top of the range Salomon trainers were not. We tried to reason with the bouncer: "Look you fascist bastard, what's wrong with them?" It didn't work. Some people just won't listen to rational argument. Then we tried some acerbic wit: "It looks like a bit of a shithole anyway." Things were beginning to get out of hand.

At this point Mark, the Ash Tree Chairman, came over to try and calm the situation but it was too late; something had upset the bouncers. "We're calling the police," they said. "It's all on CCTV you know." With armed response units being mobilised all over

Cheshire and the prospect of ten years in Strangeways looming, we decided to cut our losses. We hailed a minibus and headed back to the *Peacock*.

Having got back to the pub, Mark and Andrew announced that they refused to be dictated to by a bunch of bouncers and, singing "The boys are back in town", they set off again for the wild streets of Nantwich. Their footwear was deemed acceptable and so they were allowed into *Nakatcha*. They chatted up the fourteen-year-old girls in flip-flops and danced with the Nantwich farmers. Ash Tree honour had been satisfied.

At breakfast in the *Peacock* next morning, Crawford, our captain, reawakening memories of Ash Tree tour captains of yesteryear, was heard to say, "What time does the bar open?" I think he was after a hair of the elk that farted, or something like that. David asked for Bloody Mary but she refused to serve him. We scanned the Sunday papers but could find no mention of any major crowd disturbances in Nantwich. We then reminded ourselves that we were on a cricket tour and prepared for the impending battle against Wistaston.

Mention of a Chairman and a Captain will indicate to you that the Ash Tree is a proper cricket club with all the appropriate club positions. As well as the Chairman and Captain we have a President, a Club Secretary, a Treasurer, a Vice-Captain, a Fixture Secretary, a Social Secretary, a Press Officer, an Assistant Press Officer and a Fines Chairman. In fact, almost as many positions as we have members who pay their 'subs'. All these positions are 'democratically' elected at the AGM in November. In all the years I have played for the club, I don't remember a single contested election. The Ash Tree cricket club has more in common with a communist state than a democratically run organisation and I suspect most cricket clubs are the same. John is President for life and Mark is Chairman for life, albeit nominally elected each year.

The role of Captain is the key position. It is by a long way the most onerous job in any cricket club. It is not so much what he has to do during a match, it's the getting eleven players on to the pitch in the first place that's the difficult bit. Each year, someone will be persuaded, cajoled, blackmailed if necessary, into taking the job. This all happens before the AGM. God forbid that we should get to the AGM and not know who is going to be democratically elected to the key positions.

County cricket captains are appointed by 'the committee', so not much different to the Ash Tree really. They just don't bother with the pretence of democracy. Quite the most astonishing appointment came in 1946 when Surrey offered the captaincy to Major Nigel Bennett, by mistake. Evidently, the original choice of captain, Monty Garland-Wells, had to withdraw because his father had died. The committee decided to offer the captaincy to Major Leo Bennett, a well-known club cricketer. While this was going on, Major Nigel Bennett turned up at the Oval to renew his Surrey membership. The clerk took his papers in to the Secretary who happened to be with the Chairman and they offered Major Nigel Bennett the captaincy. He accepted!

Sir Alec Bedser called it a "cock up" and blamed it on the post war confusion at the Oval which, among other things, had been prepared for use as a prisoner-of-war camp, although never actually used as such. During an early season game, Major Bennett did not endear himself to Alf Gover, Surrey's opening bowler, when he twice rolled the new ball along the ground to him. Later, he asked Jim Laker, who had just joined Surrey, to open the bowling. When he replied that he was an off break bowler Bennett said "But you bowl quick too don't you?"

Major Bennett did manage three fifties, including 79 against Kent and scored 688 runs in the season, so he obviously knew which end to hold the bat. The Surrey players, on the whole, seemed relaxed about the situation. "I reckon we can cope with him for the summer," one apparently said. "His wife's a real cracker."

I imagine that if you have come through six years of war you are just happy to be playing some cricket instead of being shot at. Surrey finished joint 11th in the County Championship, their lowest position ever, and *Wisden,* commenting on Bennett's performance as captain, noted that "want of knowledge of county cricket on the field presented an unconquerable hindrance to the satisfactory accomplishment of arduous duties." Which I'm sure is exactly how the *Sun* would have put it if it had been around at the time. Errol Holmes, who had been captain before the war, was invited to take over for the 1947 season.

The Ash Tree captain in 2007 was Crawford. He is not normally lacking in negotiating skills but came back from the toss with the Wistaston captain to announce that local rules applied and we would be playing 40 overs per innings. We normally only play 30 overs each innings and, while ten extra overs may not sound much, several of the team were still feeling a little tired and emotional. Suffice to say, not everyone welcomed the extra overs with open arms.

Wistatston batted first and we actually did quite well to begin with, considering they seemed to have one or two Saturday league players obviously looking to improve their runs aggregate for the season. Those extra ten overs predictably took their toll and Wistaston finally ended up on 230 from their allotted overs.

After a very welcome tea to sustain us, we started our innings. It looked a tall order from the outset and so it proved. At 133 for

6 and with more than ten overs to go, the rain came to our rescue. Crawford assured us all that the alacrity with which he accepted the Wistaston's captain's offer of a draw was no reflection on his faith in the batsmen still to come.

The champagne moment of the match was shared between Joe's excellent diving catch at cover, cigarette still in mouth and Chris's imperious pull for his second consecutive boundary, the bowler having changed from gentle Sunday Taverners leg breaks to fierce Saturday league pace after the first boundary.

England had started that summer with a series win against what was arguably the worst West Indies team ever to tour this country. A long running dispute between the West Indies Cricket Board and the players was still continuing when they arrived and can not have helped the team's frame of mind. They only had one warm up match before the First Test. This was rained off and the West Indian bowlers arrived at Lords without having bowled a single ball in anger. It was Peter Moores' first Test series as England coach and he could not have asked for an easier introduction to international cricket.

Pietersen, Prior, Vaughan, Collingwood and Cook all averaged over 50. Even Sidebottom averaged 49, admittedly with the help of some 'not outs'. That Panesar should be the leading England wicket taker in a series played on the green wickets of May and June was a reflection on both the West Indies' batting and England's seam attack.

The Lords Test was a draw due to rain but England won the three remaining Tests. Shivnarine Chanderpaul was a lone beacon of resistance for the West Indies. He top scored in every innings that he played and ended with an average of 148.66 – the highest ever Test series average for an overseas batsman in England. He left Don Bradman, Steve Waugh, Viv Richards and Garry Sobers in his wake.

With the Test series over, the West Indies Cricket Board continued to do their best to disrupt their team's progress. The selectors wanted to offer the job of one-day captain to Chris Gayle. The Board rejected this initially and said they wanted Daren Ganga, who had stood in for the injured Sarwan in the Tests, to continue. Eventually Gayle was appointed but it was yet another example of mismanagement by the West Indies Board and hardly conducive to team morale.

With Chris Gayle finally in charge, the Twenty:20 series was drawn one apiece. In the first ODI, England struggled to a total of 225 but the Windies were shot out for 146. Once again Chanderpaul stood alone, with 53 not out. Somehow the West Indies managed to recover, perhaps responding to Gayle's laid back Jamaican charisma. They won both the next two games comfortably and Paul Collingwood had lost his first one-day series as captain, 2 – 1. Chanderpaul got a century in the second ODI, unbeaten of course. In the deciding game, it was difficult to know which was the more surprising: Chanderpaul being out for only 33 or Chris Gayle taking forty-two overs for his 82.

It was a season of two halves for England. The three match series against India that followed the games against the West Indies had everything. Good cricket from both sides, bouncers, beamers, barging and jelly babies.

None of the Ashes winning bowling quintet of 2005 were available for England against India. Flintoff, Harmison, Hoggard and Jones were all injured and Giles had retired. With no 'all-rounder' to take Flintoff's place, England reverted to a four man bowling attack made up of Anderson, Sidebottom, Tremlett and Panesar.

Bad light and rain ultimately thwarted England in the First Test at Lords but did not prevent it from being a very exciting game. Had Hawk-Eye been the umpire, Panesar's imploring appeal for LBW against Sreesanth would have been upheld and England would have won. As it was, Steve Bucknor turned it down and a few minutes later, the teams came off for bad light.

In the Second Test at Trent Bridge, an England player placed some jelly babies near the stumps when Zaheer Khan went out to bat. Although there was no TV footage to support it, some of the newspapers named Ian Bell as the most likely culprit. Ian Bell?! Up to that point, the general impression was that geese could confidently approach Bell without any fear of a boo. Could it really have been him and if so why did he do it?

One theory was that it was intended to wind up Zaheer Khan as there had been a number of comments about his weight. If so, it worked. He took five wickets in the second innings and India won the match. A more generous explanation was that the jelly baby was there to mark the position where short leg was supposed to stand. It was all rather puerile, or infantile you could say, and certainly didn't do England any favours.

During the same Test match, Sreesanth seemed to be on a one-man mission to rough up the England batsmen. He shoulder barged Michael Vaughan, bowled a beamer at Kevin Pietersen and overstepped by two feet to bowl a bouncer at Paul Collingwood. He was fined half his match fee for the barge and apparently given a talking to by Dravid, the Indian captain.

This is how it should be. It is part of the captain's job to set the standards for the team and if a player transgresses, then it is right that he should have a word with him. Cook missed a trick when he pretended that he hadn't heard Graeme Swann say "F**k off" to Siddique when he finally got him out in England's second Test against

Bangladesh in March 2010. Maybe Cook is an Arsenal supporter and had been taking lessons from Arsene Wenger? An Arsenal player could take out a Kalashnikov and gun down the entire opposition midfield and Wenger would say he hadn't seen it.

To Swann's credit, he apologised unreservedly afterwards. His outburst was born of tiredness and frustration having bowled 49 overs in Bangladesh's second innings. All Cook had to say was that Swann had said it in the heat of the moment and he was sure that he regretted it. If he had done that then, not only would he have maintained the moral high ground, but also shown himself to be a leader with a mind of his own. The 'Wenger approach' did him no credit.

One up and one to play, India batted first at the Oval and scored 664. All eleven batsmen reached double figures, only the eleventh time this had happened in a Test match. Despite the presence of Tendulkar, Laxman, Ganguly and Dravid, the only Indian to score a century in the match, and indeed in the series, was Anil Kumble. One of the 'nice guys' of international cricket, it was his first and only Test century in his 118th appearance for his country.

England made 345 when they batted but Dravid did not enforce the follow-on. He may have regretted it when India were 11 for 3 in their second innings but they recovered to 180 for 6 and then declared with a lead of 500. England were never likely to win but they could lose. Pietersen scored 101 and then got out but the game ended in a draw. Dravid had become only the third Indian captain to win a Test series in England.

An exciting seven match ODI series followed (it's not often you can say that) with England winning the final game to take the series 4 − 3 (and you can't say that often either!)

2007 had been a pretty good year for England considering the injuries to their first choice bowlers and adjusting to a new coach and a new ODI captain. It had also been a good year for the Ash Tree. The tour to Nantwich had helped to 'bond' the team and there was encouraging talk of enthusiasm for future tours, maybe even venturing outside Cheshire.

7. New Zealand tour of Australia, 1980/81

Diego Maradona, Zinedine Zidane, Thierry Henry and Greg Chappell were all very, very good players, arguably great players but they are all remembered predominantly for something other than outstanding ability at their chosen sport.

In the case of Maradona it is the 'Hand of God' goal against England. With Zidane it is that World Cup Final head butt and for Henry it is the handball against the Irish. And Greg Chappell? You can probably guess but we will come to him later.

I acknowledge that this is a somewhat Anglo Saxon view. Maradona and Zidane are still worshipped as gods in their respective countries. Henry can do no wrong in certain parts of North London and is a hero in France but he probably won't be holding his next stag do in Dublin. If you are an Irish Arsenal supporter, and there are a few (e.g. Dara O'Briain who appeared on the BBC's *Newsnight* accepting David Ginola'a apologies from an embarrassed French people), then you are on the horns of a genuine dilemma. Henry, is he hero or zero?

In English eyes, Diego Maradona will forever be associated with the 'Hand of God' goal that he scored for Argentina against England in the 1986 World Cup quarterfinal. How 5' 5" Maradona managed to get to the ball before 6' 1" Peter Shilton remains a mystery. As is how the Tunisian referee failed to spot Maradona's left hand punching the ball into the net. Even his teammates saw him do it; Maradona had to urge them to celebrate with him in case the referee changed his mind about awarding the goal.

Four minutes later, Maradona proceeded to dribble the ball over sixty yards, through half the England team before finally rounding Shilton and slotting the ball into the net. It was later nominated The Goal of the Century by FIFA.

Gary Lineker got a goal back from a John Barnes cross to make it 2 −1 and that was how the score stayed. For Argentina, it was revenge for the 1966 World Cup quarterfinal when they had Rattin sent off and of course it was retribution for the Falklands Conflict, which was still very fresh in the memory. Lineker's six goals in the tournament won him the coveted Golden Boot award but Argentina went on to win the World Cup.

22nd June 1986, the day of the 'Hand of God' goal, was the rest day of England's Second Test against India. England got thrashed, scoring 102 in the first innings and 128 in the second. The game took place at Leeds and *Wisden's* review of the match had this to say:

"... spectators who tried to recreate the human wave effect by synchronised waving of the arms when Azharuddin was batting on Friday afternoon. Their mindless imitation of the football crowds at the World Cup in Mexico did not help the batsman's concentration and left Headingley's reputation as a ground for cricket lovers as much in tatters as the reputation of the England team."

I am completely with *Wisden* on this. If you are ever watching a Test match on TV and you see three blokes resolutely staying in their seats as a Mexican wave goes round the ground, it will probably be Colin, Roger and me. If you then observe the same three blokes muttering obscenities to themselves and to the people standing up in front of them, it will almost certainly be us. The use of the verb 'muttering' is important. The obscenities will be loud enough for us to hear but not quite loud enough for the people in front to detect what we are actually saying.

Colin, Roger and I are in what increasingly seems to be a minority these days. We go to a Test match mainly to watch the cricket. Perverse possibly, but true. If I wanted to jump up and down in the air with lots of people I don't know, then I would join an aerobics class.

For completeness, I would also like to make it clear that I don't go to Test matches in fancy dress (unless jeans and blue denim shirt count) and I'm not a great fan of the Barmy Army either. Why would you go to a cricket match and want to listen to this sung over and over and over again?

Everywhere we go
Everywhere we go
The people want to know
The people want to know
Who we are
Who we are
Where we come from
Where we come from
Shall we tell them
Shall we tell them
Who we are
Who we are
Etc etc

While we are on the subject, I was at Edgbaston in 2009 when elements of the Barmy Army, booed Ricky Ponting as he came out to bat. Admittedly it was mainly 'good-natured' pantomime booing but it did not feel right. I'm a long way from being a member of the Ricky Ponting fan club; I want him to be clean bowled first ball but that doesn't mean I'm happy to see him booed as he goes out to bat. It is vulgar, demeaning and totally lacking in sportsmanship.

Just because Australian spectators sometimes do it to our batsmen is not a good enough reason for us to do it too. You might as well say that because some of the Pacific Islanders used to eat missionaries, it was OK for the missionaries to do the same to them. Ponting is a very, very good batsman and deserves some respect. It's the thin end of the wedge. Before we know it, cricket will have degenerated to the boorish and tedious habit of football crowds booing any visiting players they don't like.

Anyway, I digress. Just as Maradona is forever linked with the 'Hand of God' goal so Zinedine Zidane will always be remembered for his head butt in the 2006 World Cup Final. Zidane was a wonderful footballer and played with distinction for a number of clubs including Juventus and Real Madrid. Just before he signed for Juventus from Bordeaux, the Blackburn Rovers manager, Ray Harford, expressed an interest in signing him. Jack Walker, the owner of Blackburn Rovers, apparently replied: "Why do you want to sign Zidane when we have Tim Sherwood?"

Zidane played for France 108 times. He scored two goals in the 1998 World Cup Final when France beat Brazil 3 − 0. Eight years later, the 2006 World Cup Final was to be his last professional appearance. It started well for him when he opened the scoring with a penalty, given away by Marco Materazzi. Italy equalised through none other than Marco Materazzi and the game went to extra time.

Materazzi, making a strong bid for the man of the match award, then made his most significant contribution to the game. He tugged Zidane's shirt and apparently Zidane said that if he wanted his shirt that much he would give it to him after the match. As Zidane walked away, Materazzi can be seen saying something. It obviously wasn't complimentary because Zidane calmly turned round and head butted Materazzi in the chest, knocking him to the ground.

The referee didn't see it but a quarter of a billion viewers and the fourth official did. Zidane was sent off and Italy went on to win the match on penalties. Just to rub it in, Materazzi was one of Italy's successful penalty takers.

There was much speculation as to what Materazzi had said to provoke the attack by France's captain and winner of the player of the tournament award. The immediate post match favourite was that Materazzi had called Zidane, whose parents were born in Algeria, a terrorist. A few years later, Materazzi revealed that when Zidane had offered him his shirt, he had replied "I'd prefer your whore of a sister." Not particularly pleasant but hardly enough to provoke a flying head butt you would have thought.

As an interesting contrast to when David Beckham was vilified and denounced for his sending off against Argentina in 1998, Zidane was seemingly forgiven by most of the French supporters. President Jacques Chirac said after the match: "You are a virtuoso, a genius of world football. You are also a man of the heart, of commitment, of conviction, and that's why France admires and loves you."

Not everyone was so forgiving. "With one blow, the icon is smashed," wrote *Le Monde* in its editorial. *Liberation* offered its readers this sobering thought: "For a month, France has dreamed alongside Zidane. This morning, it woke up with Chirac."

Maradona and Zidane, both football geniuses, will forever be remembered for acts of ungentlemanly conduct. So too will Thierry Henry for his instinctive (French view) or deliberate (view of everybody not French) handball, not once but twice in the World Cup qualifier against Ireland in 2009. An awful lot of negative karma must have followed Henry and the French team to South Africa. The captaincy was taken away from Henry, he didn't start any of the matches and the French were a shambles. The squad imploded spectacularly and finished with more strikers than Maradona's Argentina team. France finished bottom of their group and went home in disgrace.

You may be forgiven for thinking that this is supposed to be a book about cricket and this chapter is supposed to be about Greg Chappell and New Zealand's tour to Australia in 1980/81. Well yes it is but I would claim the C.L.R. James defence. What do they know of cricket who only cricket know?

Handballs and head butts in football matches possibly aren't what James had in mind but it can be salutary to look at what can happen in the heat of the battle in other sports. Maradona's act, and his lack of regret, is not altogether surprising given his reputation both on and off the pitch during his career. Zidane had 'previous' as his sending off in the World Cup Final was the fourteenth of his career. He apologised for his action but said he did not regret it. In a way, it is admirable that Zidane should put the honour of his sister above a mere soccer match. It's just a shame for him it happened to be the World Cup Final. However, his exemplary life off the pitch probably helped him maintain his reputation after he retired, despite arguably costing his country a second World Cup.

Mention 'the underarm incident' to most cricket followers and they will immediately think of either Greg Chappell, or his younger brother Trevor, or maybe even older brother Ian who was commentating on the match. Certainly there was a cacophony of Chappells around at the time.

The incident happened towards the end of New Zealand's tour of Australia in the winter of 1980/81. There has always been fierce rivalry between the two countries and had this incident happened in the 18th century, it could easily have led to war. If you think that seems far-fetched then it is worth remembering the War of Jenkin's Ear. In 1739, Britain declared war on Spain because the captain of a British merchant ship, Captain Robert Jenkins, had his ear cut off by the Spanish, eight years earlier.

The New Zealand squad that arrived in Australia at the end of October 1980 was a capable one. Although Glenn Turner, their best batsman, did not make himself available for the tour, they still had a competitive team. Edgar and Wright were an experienced opening pair. Geoff Howarth, the captain, had developed into a fine batsman while playing for Surrey. Coney and Burgess were promising players and Richard Hadlee was well on his way to becoming a world class all-rounder.

Any New Zealand team has to overcome a slight inferiority complex when playing their 'big brother' at cricket. They did not do themselves justice in the three Test matches and lost the series 2 – 0. They would have to wait till 1985 before they recorded their first ever Test win on Australian soil. When the time arrived they did it in style, winning by an innings and 41 runs. Richard Hadlee took 15 wickets in the match, 9 for 52 in the first innings and 6 for 71 in the second. Martin Crowe and John Reid got centuries. For good measure they went on to win the series 2 – 1.

However, that was all in the future. In 1980, they had been outplayed in the Tests but still had high hopes of doing well in the Triangular one-day series. India were eliminated after a multitude of preliminary matches, which started in November and carried on till January. New Zealand went through with Australia to compete in the *Benson & Hedges* World Series Cup Finals, on a best of five games basis.

New Zealand won the first match at Sydney, helped by an excellent innings from John Wright, well supported by Geoff Howarth. Five wickets for Hadlee saw a rather complacent Australia fall short by 78 runs. New Zealand's batting failed in the second match, played in Melbourne, and Australia won comfortably by 7 wickets.

The third match, played once again at the MCG, was to be one of the most talked about games in the history of cricket. The major controversy, which nearly did result in a declaration of war, revolved around the last ball of the match. However, earlier in the game, there had been another episode that was somewhat overlooked because of the brouhaha at the end. The New Zealanders were certainly not laughing.

Australia batted first and Greg Chappell on 52, refused to walk when Sneddon, at deep mid-wicket, claimed what appeared to be a low but fair catch. Both umpires somewhat bizarrely said that they were looking for short runs rather than watching the ball so couldn't give Chappell out. It was left to the batsman to accept Sneddon's word, strongly supported by Howarth. Chappell declined to do this, although subsequent television pictures proved conclusively that it was a fair catch.

Greg Chappell went on to score 90 and Australia made 235 off their 50 overs. In the days before disputed catches were referred to the third umpire, it was the convention to accept the fielder's word. Chappell was effectively saying that he thought Sneddon was cheating. In fact it was Chappell who was 'cheating' by not walking when he was out. Had he done so then Australia may not have scored as many as they did and he would not have had the albatross of the 'underarm incident' round his neck for the rest of his days. What goes around, comes around.

When New Zealand batted they got to the last over requiring 15 runs to win. A very fine undefeated 102 from Bruce Edgar had helped them get to this position but he wasn't facing when the last over started. Greg Chappell's younger brother, Trevor, was given the responsibility of bowling it. The first ball was hit for 4 by Richard Hadlee, who was then out LBW to the next one. A young, slim-line Ian Smith, the Kiwi wicket-keeper, replaced Hadlee. He hit the next couple of balls for 2 runs each and was then bowled heaving across the line to a ball that kept low.

Brian McKechnie, the fast medium bowler who also played 26 times for the rugby All Blacks, came out to face the last ball. He was not renowned for his batting and he had to hit his first ball for a six just to tie the match. At this point, Greg Chappell's brain went into meltdown. He came over to his brother and instructed him to bowl the last ball underarm along the ground.

There was general disbelief around the ground when people realised what was about to happen. You can watch the entire last over on *YouTube* and very entertaining it is too. Rod Marsh, who was keeping wicket for Australia, can be seen shaking his head and clearly indicating that he does not approve. Even Ian Chappell, who was commentating on the game, says "No, Greg, no, you can't do that".

The captain of a cricket team has more power and responsibility than the captain of any other sports team. He decides who bowls, what field to set (unless S.F. Barnes or Ian Botham is bowling), what the batting order should be, and is generally in charge in a way that football and rugby captains are not. So, when Greg told his brother to bowl underarm, Trevor really had no choice. He could have tried to persuade him against it, I suppose, but being the younger sibling probably didn't help in that regard.

Chappell junior duly rolled the ball along the ground. McKechnie blocked it and then threw his bat in the air in disgust. He was subsequently censured for bringing the game into disrepute for doing this. Who says the ICC hasn't got a sense of humour?

Australia had won but most of the 50,000, predominantly Australian crowd, booed as the players came off the pitch. The climax of a great game of cricket had been snatched away from them. Replays later showed that it was technically a no ball because Dennis Lillee had forgotten to walk in to his correct fielding place and so Australia had one too many players outside the inner fielding circle. In the excitement the umpires, understandably perhaps, had not noticed.

The repercussions were immediate. It seems that nobody apart from Greg Chappell thought that what he did was a good idea. The Prime Minister of New Zealand, Robert Muldoon, didn't beat about the bush. He described it as "the most disgusting incident I can recall in the history of cricket". For good measure he went on to say that "it was an act of true cowardice and I consider it appropriate that the Australian team were wearing yellow."

Even the Australian Prime Minister, Malcolm Fraser, called the act "contrary to the traditions of the game". Sir Donald Bradman "totally disapproved" of what had happened. Commentating for *Channel 9* at the time, Richie Benaud described the act as "disgraceful" and said it was "one of the worst things I have ever seen done on a cricket field". Harold Larwood, aged seventy-seven at the time and living in retirement in Sydney, probably summed it up best when he said that it was "a bloody stupid thing to do.'"

So, that's his older brother, Rod Marsh, 50,000 Australian spectators, two Prime Ministers, Sir Don Bradman, the esteemed Richie, Harold Larwood and probably the Pope and the Duke of Edinburgh all indicating their disapproval of Greg Chappell. If he felt under pressure during the game, heaven knows what he must have felt like in the immediate aftermath.

In my view, it could all have been avoided if the umpires had had the presence of mind to invoke the Laws of Cricket, as laid down at the time.

Law 42 covers Unfair Play in the game of cricket:

42 (1) is concerned with the 'Responsibilities of Captains' and specifies: "The captains are responsible at all times for ensuring that play is conducted within the spirit of the game as well as within the Laws."

Well, it seems pretty obvious that Greg Chappell had broken that rule by saying to the umpire that the last ball would be bowled underarm.

42 (2) deals with the 'Responsibilities of Umpires' and states: "The umpires are the sole judges of fair and unfair play."

A blind man could see that what Greg Chappell instructed his brother to do was "unfair play", so one would hope the umpires could have spotted it.

42 (3) 'Intervention by the Umpire' empowers the officials with: "The umpires shall intervene without appeal, by calling and signalling 'Dead ball' in the case of unfair play."

The umpires could, and should, have called 'dead ball' when Trevor Chappell rolled the ball along the ground.

There you have it. All the umpire had to do was say to Greg, 'Look mate, this isn't on. It's unfair play, it's against the spirit of the game and it's contrary to Law 42.' Had the umpire done that, nobody would have complained about his decision and both Greg and Trevor Chappell would have been spared the burden of carrying the 'underarm incident' around with them for the rest of their lives.

The latest version of the very comprehensive Laws of Cricket (they take up fifty pages in *Wisden*), now has a new section at the beginning called The Preamble. It sets out to define The Spirit of Cricket and is quite clear that the major responsibility for ensuring the spirit of fair play lies with the captains. The umpires' job is to intervene where necessary.

The updated clarification of what is meant by the 'spirit of cricket' didn't stop Paul Colllingwood not quite getting the hang of it in 2008. The opposition were ...... New Zealand! The incident took place at the Oval during the 4th ODI. New Zealand were chasing England's fairly modest total of 245 when Ryan Sidebottam collided with Grant Elliott, who was going for a quick single. Although it's tempting to speculate that England's Mr Angry deliberately took out Elliott, in fact the collision was completely accidental.

Grant Elliott was knocked to the ground. The ball was thrown to the bowler's end and Elliott was run out. Collingwood, who was captain, later said that he had to make a "split second decision". That's not quite right as the umpire, Mark Benson, asked him if he was absolutely sure that he wanted to uphold the appeal. Collingwood thought about it, said yes and so Elliott had to go. There were boos from many sections of the crowd. I remember watching the game on television at the time and hoping that New Zealand would go on to win. Luckily for Collingwood they did, off the last ball of the match. The England captain could not have asked Luke Wright to roll the last ball along the ground even if he had wanted to. This action had been outlawed immediately following the match in 1981.

To Collingwood's credit he did apologise immediately after the match when he had had time to reflect on what he had done. It wasn't quite in the same league as Greg Chappell's underarm incident but shows what can happen when a player is under pressure. Collingwood simply made the wrong decision. Chappell's action, on the other hand, was premeditated and tantamount to cheating, even though it was technically within the laws of the game, Law 42 notwithstanding!

Collingwood gave up the one day captaincy soon afterwards but the following year, during the Champions Trophy in South Africa, he was to be embroiled in yet another 'spirit of cricket' controversy, once again with New Zealand. Why are New Zealand always involved?

During their Group match, Collingwood received a vicious delivery from Kyle Mills that reared off a length and went through to the keeper. Collingwood glanced at the square leg umpire and took a couple of steps down the wicket to examine the spot where the ball had pitched. Brendon McCullum then threw down the stumps. Collingwood was clearly out of his ground but there was some dispute as to whether umpire Daryl Harper had called for the end of the over. As it was Daryl, he probably wasn't sure whether he had either.

Considering what had happened at the Oval fifteen months earlier, the Kiwis could be forgiven for wanting to get some revenge. What goes around, comes around. Collingwood obviously wasn't trying to go for a run but he was out of his crease. After some discussion, Daniel Vettori, the New Zealand captain, showed that he at least did understand what is meant by the 'spirit of cricket' and withdrew the appeal. Collingwood went on to top score with 40 but New Zealand won the match. The 'good guys' had won both times.

New Zealand have not always been the 'good guys'. In 2006, Brendon McCullum ran out Muttiah Muralitharan when he left his crease to congratulate Kumar Sangakkara on scoring a century. The ball was not 'dead' so he was within his rights. The captain, Stephen Fleming, could have called Muralitharan back but chose not to. New Zealand went on to win the match.

The so-called 'spirit of cricket' is difficult to define but usually easy to spot if it is broken. At the start of the third Ashes Test at Edgbaston in 2009, Australia's wicket-keeper, Brad Haddin, broke a finger in the thirty minutes between the toss and start of play. Ricky Ponting, had nominated the team in writing before the toss, so a replacement could be allowed only with the England captain's consent. By the laws of the game, Strauss did not have to let Australia bring in a new keeper but he did and it felt the right thing to do. The 'spirit of cricket' was upheld. Graham Manou was the grateful beneficiary and went on to make his début.

The main reason why the underarm incident in the New Zealand versus Australia match is still talked about to this day is that what happened was so manifestly against the 'spirit of cricket' that it was obvious to all and sundry, except Greg Chappell. So why did he do it?

Although his immediate reaction was to say that it was within the rules, he soon apologised and has been apologising for it ever since. Given the torrent of condemnation that engulfed him, he had little choice. Some years later Chappell's defence, or explanation, was that he felt that he was having some sort of physical and mental breakdown.

It was the beginning of the new professional era for Australian cricket following Kerry Packer's World Series Cricket. There were a lot of problems to sort out including scheduling of games, contracts and playing conditions. As Australia's captain, Greg

Chappell was involved in all of this and things had just got too much for him.

The pressure of non-stop cricket had taken its toll. When coupled with all the off field activities that he was involved with, Chappell was no longer enjoying the game at which he excelled. In the back of his mind, as his brother began to bowl that last over, was the thought that if Australia won the third One-Day Final they would only have to win one more game to clinch the series. If Australia went 3 – 1 up, the last game would not have to be played. He did not want to take the risk of the third game ending up a tie and having to play yet another game.

Australia did indeed go on to win the fourth game, relatively easily. Greg Chappell, booed to the wicket as he went out to bat but then cheered as he went off having scored 87, was named Man of the Finals. Australia had won the series 3 – 1 and the fifth and final game was not required.

So, what to make of the enigma that was Greg Chappell? As a batsman, Chappell was a class act. John Arlott was of the view that, "for most of the 1970s, Greg Chappell was probably the best batsman in the world." He was a tall, stylish, right handed batsman, particularly strong on the leg-side, which included a highly individualistic shot off his hips from a very upright stance. He inherited the Australian captaincy from his brother, Ian, in 1975 and tried to raise the standards of dress and behaviour that had deteriorated somewhat during his brother's reign. Greg Chappell was conscientious and demanding, acquiring the nickname of 'the major general'. And yet, ironically, it is he that is associated with a famous act of bad sportsmanship not his more raucous aggressive older brother.

Greg Chappell scored over 7,000 Test runs for Australia, including 24 centuries, at an average of nearly 54. His Test average puts him in the same bracket as Tendulkar, Lara and Ponting of recent players and slightly ahead of Viv Richards and Sunil Gavaskar who were his contemporaries. He was an outstanding slip fielder and took 122 catches in his eighty-seven Tests. At the start of his career, Chappell spent two summers at Somerset and developed his skills in the county game, as many overseas players began to do around that time. Although primarily a batsman, Chappell went to Somerset as an occasional leg spinner but came back a very useful medium pacer.

After the controversial series against New Zealand, Greg Chappell chose not to go on the next tour with the Australian team, which was to England. The furore over the underarm incident may well have played a part in his decision. Had he toured England in 1981, it is reasonable to assume that the epic Botham/Willis Headingley Test match would never have happened in quite the way it did. So you could say that some good did come out of Chappell's decision to ask his brother to bowl that underarm ball.

8. West Indies tour of Australia, 1960/61

Although George Headley had captained the West Indies for one Test in 1948, no black man had been appointed as captain of the Caribbean Islands cricket team for a series prior to 1960. This despite the fact that the West Indies had been blessed with the three Ws who had dominated their cricket from the late 1940s through to the late 1950s. Frank Worrell, Everton Weekes and Clyde Walcott were born within eighteen months of each other and all within a couple of miles of the Kensington Oval, Bridgetown in Barbados. They were all great players by any standard but none of them had captained the West Indies at cricket.

Frank Worrell had been Jeffrey Stollmeyer's vice captain in the 1953/54 home series against England. However, in the next series against Australia, Denis Atkinson, a white Bajan, had replaced Worrell. As it turned out, Atkinson had to captain in three of the Tests when Stollmeyer was injured. Atkinson was an inexperienced captain and not in the same class as Worrell, Weekes and Walcott, who were all in the side, but had the disadvantage of being black. Atkinson was also appointed as captain for the tour to New Zealand which was to take place a year later, with another white man, Bruce Pairaudean, as his vice captain.

Clyde Walcott, in his book *Island Cricketers*, had a generous explanation for these decisions. The three Ws all played League cricket in Lancashire, and were therefore professionals. Walcott reckoned that the West Indies Cricket Board wanted an amateur captain, as was the tradition in England until 1952. In that year, Len Hutton was appointed captain of England despite the misgivings of some of the English cricket establishment. Hutton wasn't black but he was a professional.

The captaincy was further complicated by inter-island rivalry. The islands of the West Indies were all individual territories, each with their own government and culture. They came together for the purposes of cricket but otherwise were very independent. With Hall and Griffith to open the bowling and the three Ws supported by Sobers and Hunte, Barbados could probably have put out a team to match any country in the world, but that's another matter.

Colonial rule was coming to an end in the 1950s. Two of the bigger islands, Jamaica and Trinidad, were moving towards independence.[13] Black men were moving into positions of power and authority in government and commerce, but the captain of the West Indies cricket team remained a white prerogative. This was patently absurd and not sustainable.

Maintaining that only a white man can captain the West Indies at cricket is a bit like saying only an old Etonian can be Prime Minister of Britain[14]. It doesn't mean to say that the successful candidate can't do a good job, it's just that it does rather restrict the possible applicants. John Goddard, initially, was a popular and successful captain particularly when he led the West Indies to their first series victory in England, in 1950. However, when he was brought out of virtual retirement to lead the team to England again in 1957, there was discontent and discord in the touring party. The West

13 Both finally achieved independence from the United Kingdom in 1962. Barbados was a little later, in 1966.

14 David Cameron was the nineteenth Old Etonian to become Prime Minister when he got the job in May 2010. Compare this to no Prime Ministers ever coming from, for instance, Fallibroome High School in Macclesfield.

Indies lost three of the Tests by an innings and the other two were 'losing draws'. It was not a happy side and this was reflected in their performances.

In fact, Frank Worrell had been offered the captaincy twice. Once for the home series against Pakistan in 1957/58 and again for the tour to India and Pakistan in 1958/59. He turned both down as he was studying for his degree in England. Significantly, neither he, nor any other black player, had been given the opportunity to captain against the two most prestigious (and white) cricketing countries – England and Australia.

While Worrell was studying for his degree in Manchester, Gerry Alexander, a white Jamaican and a Cambridge cricket blue, captained the West Indies to India and Pakistan in 1958/59. They beat India but Roy Gilchrist, the volatile fast bowler, was sent home for disciplinary reasons. The second leg of the tour against Pakistan was lost.

Alexander was the Windies wicket-keeper and a useful lower middle order batsman. He had expected Worrell to take over as captain for the visit of the MCC[15] to the Caribbean in 1959/60. The West Indies Board persuaded him to carry on, and this did not go down well with the majority of the cricket loving population.

The series started in Barbados with a draw. Worrell scored 197 not out and shared in a West Indies record fourth wicket partnership of 399 with Sobers. It was during the Second Test in Trinidad that C.L.R. James, the author of *Beyond a Boundary*, started a campaign to have Worrell appointed as captain for the forthcoming tour to Australia.

James was a revolutionary Marxist who enjoyed reading Shakespeare, Thackeray and Dickens; a cricket lover who didn't see a Test match for fifteen years while living in the United States.

15 Until the mid-1970s the official England touring team played as the MCC.

He was a friend of various luminaries including such disparate figures as Sir Learie Constantine, Jomo Kenyatta and Edith Sitwell. He returned to Trinidad, the island of his birth, in 1958 to edit the political newspaper *The Nation*. James used this as the platform for his campaign to make Frank Worrell the first black captain of the West Indies. His arguments were on purely cricketing grounds. He did not make colour an explicit issue; he didn't have to.

On the third day of the Second Test at Trinidad there was a riot, with bottles being thrown on to the field. The catalyst was when Singh, a local player in his first Test match, was adjudged run out. None of the rioting, or bottles, was aimed at the English players but play was interrupted. The underlying causes among the 30,000 crowd included the oppressive heat, unhappiness with the West Indies batting performance (they were 98 − 8 when the players had to leave the field) and a general discontent exacerbated by the writings of James.

England went on to win the Second Test and the series, with the remaining three matches being drawn. As wicket-keeper, Alexander had an outstanding series with 23 dismissals. He was by and large a popular captain with the West Indies team and some were unhappy with James's editorials in *The Nation*, even if they sympathised with them. Worrell was phlegmatic about the campaign and did not involve himself directly.

Alexander made himself available to captain the tour to Australia but said that he was equally happy to play under Worrell whom he liked and respected. He also acknowledged the difficulty of captaining and keeping wicket at the same time. The West Indies Board met and debated the issue for two full days before announcing that Worrell would be captain and Alexander vice-captain.

At the age of thirty-five, Frank Worrell became the first black man to lead the West Indies cricket team in a series. A huge amount rested on his shoulders. Success would show the world in general, and the West Indies Cricket Board in particular, that a black man could lead the West Indies. Failure would give succour to the doubters and possibly set back West Indian cricket for years.

C.L.R. James had also hoped to get Roy Gilchrist reinstated into the West Indies squad. Gilchrist looked to Worrell for advice and guidance and saw him almost as a father figure. James thought that Worrell could encourage him to apologise for his misdemeanours in India and get him rehabilitated back into the team. This didn't happen and James had to settle for a part in helping to get Worrell appointed as the West Indies cricket captain.

The Australian tour did not start particularly well for Worrell. He was suffering from food poisoning when his opposite captain, Richie Benaud, met him at the airport. In their first two state games, the West Indies lost to Western Australia and drew against South Australia. Next, they comfortably beat Victoria thanks to a double century from Rohan Kanhai and the spin bowling of Ramadhin and Valentine.

The West Indies then lost by an innings to a strong New South Wales side captained by Benaud. Worrell scored 51 in the first innings but then pulled a leg muscle and didn't bat in the second. He missed the drawn match against Queensland, the last game before the Tests began.

Although Weekes and Walcott had retired from Test cricket, a new generation of West Indian batsmen was coming through. As well as Kanhai, Worrell could call on the reliable Conrad Hunte and the incomparable Garry Sobers. Wes Hall was developing into a fearsome fast bowler and Lance Gibbs, the off-spinner, was just starting out on his career. He replaced Ramadhin in the Test side for the last three matches.

So, Worrell was blessed with talented players in the squad but could he get them playing as a team and not just a group of skilful individuals? Worrell was probably past his best as a batsman but he still made runs at key times in the series, batting at number 5. He also usually opened the bowling with Hall but it was his contribution as captain that was unique.

The memorable series started in Brisbane with one of the most exciting Tests ever played. It was variously described at the time as 'The Greatest Test Match', 'The Greatest Cricket Match' and even 'The Greatest Game ever played with a ball'. Pretty impressive billing and not a bad way for Worrell to begin his Test captaincy!

The West Indies batted first and were soon 65 for 3 with Cammie Smith, Hunte and Kanhai all falling to Alan Davidson in an exhilarating first hour; at which point Worrell came to the wicket and provided Sobers with the calmness and support that allowed him to blossom. Sobers completely dominated the Australian bowling. He had the knack, when in form, that all great players have of dispatching the good ball to the boundary. His century came in just over two hours. Sobers received a standing ovation from the crowd and was also warmly congratulated by Benaud and the Australian players. Many regard it as the best of his 26 Test centuries.

In those days, the new ball was taken after 200 runs and it was only twenty-five past two when Davidson and Meckiff had the opportunity to take it. This was in stark contrast to the previous Test match played at Brisbane, in December 1958, when Trevor 'Barnacle' Bailey batted for seven and half hours for 68. Bailey and Co clearly did not believe that they were there to entertain the paying spectators. The daily run totals for the first four days of that Ashes Test were 142, 148, 122 and 106!

Thankfully, Worrell and Benaud's approach was completely different. The whole series was played in a wonderfully positive spirit by both teams. They did not see winning and entertaining as mutually exclusive.

Neither Sobers nor Worrell were troubled by the new ball until Sobers was out to possibly the worst delivery of the day. Sobers contrived to hit a wide, leg-side full toss from Meckiff into the hands of Kline at mid-on. He paused at the wicket for some time, unable to believe that he had played such a shot, and then was applauded all the way back to the dressing room. He had stroked 21 boundaries in his 132. Jack Fingleton described it as "an immortal innings".

As is often the way with long partnerships, Worrell followed him soon afterwards. He made 65 in just over two and half hours and had been the perfect foil for Sobers. Joe Solomon had replaced Sobers and, with a correctness and wisdom appropriate to his name, also scored 65. He was out just before the end to Bobby Simpson, a part-time leg-spinner and the West Indies ended the day on 359 for 7.

Australia would have anticipated bowling the Windies out fairly quickly the next day. Benaud opened with Davidson and obviously did not expect to need him to take a second new ball, which was due if the score reached 400. Things went to plan when Ramadhin was soon out but Alexander and Hall had other ideas. Wes Hall batted rather in the style of a more successful version of Devon Malcolm. Frank Worrell had suggested a change to his grip when seeing him bat in the nets, and Hall began to put it into practice. He scored exactly 50 in a blistering partnership of 86 with Alexander.

One over from Meckiff went for 19 and Benaud reflected afterwards that 19 was exactly the number of runs scored in one pre-lunch session in the England versus Australia Test match at

Brisbane two years earlier. Benaud also reported hearing an Australian wit shout from the crowd at the end of the same over 'Eh Benaud, which one of those blokes is Sobers?'

Gerry Alexander was out for 60 soon after Hall, and the West Indies innings ended on 453. Wes Hall told his captain that he could have got a century but had deliberately got himself stumped once he had got to 50 as he needed to conserve his energy to bowl. Worrell's reaction is not recorded but neither he nor Hall could get an early breakthrough when they opened the bowling. Australia made steady progress and eventually got a first innings lead of 52, thanks mainly to a cautious 92 from Bob Simpson and an increasingly confident 181 from Norman O'Neill.

The West Indies only managed 284 the second time around, Worrell top scoring with 65. Alan Davidson took 6 for 87 giving him 11 wickets in the match. Together with his attractive 44 in Australia's first innings, he was already one of the candidates for man of the match.

Australia only needed 233 to win. They were soon 7 for 2 and then 57 for 5. Wes Hall charged in and bowled twelve eight-ball overs[16] in a row. He was exhausted but had taken four of the wickets to fall. Ramadhin and Valentine would surely finish the Australians off? Ramadhin bowled Mackay and, at 92 for 6, Benaud joined Alan Davidson at the wicket. They managed to get to tea without further loss but a West Indies victory looked a certainty.

After tea, Benaud and Davidson moved the score along. The West Indies bowling attack, including Sobers mixing his medium quick stuff with slow spin, could not get the breakthrough. The

16 Since the 1979/80 season, all Test cricket has been six ball overs. Before that, the number of balls per over varied from four or five per over in the nineteenth century to six or eight per over on the twentieth century. Different countries adopted a different number of balls per over until it was standardised in 1979.

Australian batsmen were taking any number of quick singles and the West Indies fielding was looking ragged. Worrell remained calm throughout and urged his men to relax but concentrate. It is not always easy to do both of these things at the same time in such circumstances!

With an hour to go, Australia needed 60 runs to win. The West Indies needed 4 wickets. With half an hour to go, Australia needed 27 to win. The West Indies still needed 4 wickets. The 200 was up so Worrell played his last card. The new ball was taken and Wes Hall brought back for one last effort. Despite some near misses and run out scares, Benaud and Davidson held firm.

Sobers started the penultimate over with Australia needing 9 runs to win. They ran two quick singles and then Benaud pushed a delivery wide of square leg and called for a run. Soloman pounced on the ball and threw down the wickets in one action. Davidson was run out for 80, a fantastic innings to go with his 11 wickets and first knock of 44.

Wally Grout, taking Davidson's place, had the strike and got a single off the seventh ball. Unless Benaud could get a single himself, Grout would have to face the start of the last over from Hall. Sobers bowled a perfect length and Benaud could not get it away. The last over of the last day began at four minutes to six. All four results were still possible. Australia needed six runs to win. The West Indies needed three wickets to win. A draw and a tie were also still in contention.

Wes Hall charged in and sent down the first ball of the over. It reared off a length and hit Grout on the thigh. Most professional footballers would have gone down in a heap, cried for their mummy and demanded that the perpetrator be sent off. With the ball at his feet, Grout looked up and saw Benaud rushing down the wicket. Grout did the only sensible thing. He got up and ran down the other end. Australia had sneaked a single and, more importantly for them, Benaud was on strike.

Seven balls to go, 5 runs to win, 3 wickets to win.

Hall trudged slowly back to his mark. Worrell had expressly told him not to bowl any bouncers. He ran in at pace and let go .... a bouncer. Benaud was tempted, got a touch and Alexander took the catch. The Australian captain had scored a magnificent 52 in just over two hours but he could no longer influence the game.

Six balls to go, 5 runs to win, 2 wickets to win.

Ian Meckiff came in next and played a straight bat to his first ball. No run.

Five balls to go, 5 runs to win, 2 wickets to win.

Hall's next ball went down the leg-side to the keeper. As it went past Meckiff, Grout called him for a run. Meckiff had little option but to respond. Hall had followed through down the pitch and Alexander threw the ball to him. Hall turned and shied at the stumps at the bowler's end. Had he hit, Meckiff would have been out. The ball missed and Australia had gained another run.

Four balls to go, 4 runs to win, 2 wickets to win.

There were only 4,000 spectators in the ground but they were delirious with excitement. The next ball, Grout went for a big hit to try and win the match. He mistimed his stroke and the ball spooned up somewhere between mid-wicket and square leg. At least four West Indies fielders could have taken the catch. Kanhai was under the ball ready to catch it when Wes Hall charged in, knocked him out of the way and jumped up to take the catch. The ball spilled out of his hands and Australia, instead of losing a wicket, had gained another run.

Three balls to go, 3 runs to win, 2 wickets to win.

Hall was distraught. He later said it was one of the worst moments of his life and you could well believe it. Frank Worrell showed no sign of annoyance, put his arm round his shoulders and told him to relax. Without Worrell's calming influence, Hall would have been in pieces and probably found it difficult to even run up and bowl.

As it was, he put everything into the next ball and Meckiff swung at it. He connected and it went at speed towards the square leg boundary. A four would have won the match for Australia. If they could run three that would do as well. The ball held up in the grass and Conrad Hunte raced round to collect it. As Grout was coming back for the third run to win the game, Hunte's throw from 90 yards was perfect. It had to be. Alexander took the throw cleanly and broke the wicket. Grout hurled himself full length but was out by a foot. The scores were level.

Two balls to go, 1 run to win, 1 wicket to tie.

Australia's No.11, Lindsay Kline, replaced Grout. The atmosphere was so tense that even Trevor Bailey might have been excited. Kline worked his first ball to leg and both batsmen ran. Joe Solomon swooped in from mid-wicket, picked up the ball one handed and, with only one stump to aim at, threw down the wicket. The umpire's finger went up and the game was tied, the first Test match ever to end this way.[17]

An extraordinary finish to an extraordinary Test match. The favourites to win the game changed throughout the game from session to session, hour to hour and in the final few overs, from ball to ball.

Thankfully they didn't have the ubiquitous, superfluous, plethoric man of the match awards back then (they are a bit silly aren't they?) If they had, then I would not have wanted to be the judge. There were at least eight very strong contenders. Maybe

17 A second tied Test occurred in September 1986, in Chennai, between India and Australia.

the award should have gone to the umpires? They remained composed throughout the game and refreshingly neutral. This, of course, was in the time before 'independent' umpires were appointed. The last four wickets to fall were three close run outs and a faint touch to the keeper. No need for referrals to a third umpire in those days!

The match was a huge credit to the two captains, Worrell and Benaud. Both were trying to win throughout the five days, with no thoughts of playing for a draw. Before the Tests started, they had both promised to play attacking cricket with the aim, at all times, of forcing a result. Benaud was supported in this attitude by his Chairman of Selectors, Sir Don Bradman. At tea on the last day, Australia had 124 to get in 120 minutes with only the tailenders to come after Benaud and Davidson. It was not a strong position, but during the interval Bradman asked Benaud: "What are you going for Richie, a win or a draw?" "We're going for a win, of course," replied the captain. "I am very pleased to hear it." said The Don.

The match was a tie but cricket was the winner. Cliché spotters may groan when reading this but it really was true. The game of cricket was revitalised by the positive approach of both teams. Test cricket in general and batting in particular had drifted into a very defensive and negative frame of mind during the mid and late 1950s. In 1956, for example, P.E. Richardson had scored the slowest Test century ever, in eight hours and eight minutes, for England against South Africa. Then D.J. McGlew went one better (or worse depending on your point of view) by taking just over nine hours to score a century for South Africa against Australia in 1958.

When you add in performances such as Bailey's two hours for 8 runs against South Africa in 1955 and his seven and a half hours for 68 against Australia in 1958, it was hardly surprising that cricket followers were getting bored and starting to look elsewhere for their entertainment.

The West Indies and Australia had added an extra dimension to Test cricket with the first match of the 1960/61 series and brought the crowds back to the game. It seemed that spectators enjoyed watching the flashing cover drive of Garry Sobers rather more than the forward defensive prod of Trevor Bailey.

The Second Test attracted large crowds to Melbourne. Australia had won the toss and chosen to bat. They scored 348 on the first day at more than 5 runs an over. There was just time for Solomon, Hunte's new opening partner, to be out for a duck and the West Indies ended the day at 1 for 1.

After the early loss of Hunte, Seymour Nurse and Rohan Kanhai took the score to 108 for 2 when play on the second day ended because of rain. On the third day, Kanhai was out when the total was 124, having made 84 of the runs. Nurse, restraining his normal aggressive stroke play, made a painstaking 70 but the tail folded easily and the West Indies were all out for 181.

In those days the 'follow-on' deficit in Test matches was 150 and Benaud invited the West Indies to bat again. They had reached 97 – 2 when Johnny Martin, playing in his first of only eight Tests, took the wickets of Kanhai, Sobers and Worrell in the space of four balls. Hunte and Alexander survived till the end of play. On the fourth day, Hunte made 110 and Alexander 72 but no one else contributed much and the West Indies were all out for 233. Australia only needed 67 to win and they got them with the loss of 3 wickets.

It was a tremendous anti-climax for the West Indians after the excitement and euphoria of the First Test. Worrell's captaincy was once again put to the test. Past West Indies teams might have felt demoralised and allowed it to affect their performance. Worrell's captaincy style was one of calm authority. He encouraged discussion and players making their point of view known. This was something new for West Indian cricketers.

C.L.R. James had a number of discussions with Worrell when he returned from the tour, and was struck by these words from him: "If something was wrong I told them what was right and left it to them." This surely was the key to his captaincy. Most captains can, and will, say what is going wrong. Some will also say what should be done to rectify a situation. Very few will then leave it to the players to put what is required into practice themselves.

West Indian cricketers had been used to being told what to do, following orders in other words. How much stronger and more personally satisfying it is if the leader that you respect lays down what he wants to happen and leaves it to you to actually do it.

Whether an individual was a team player or not was very important to Worrell. So was discipline on the field. During an early tour match, Sobers was adjudged LBW. He did not think he was out and showed his disagreement. Worrell was at the non-strikers end and indicated his displeasure with the dissent shown by Sobers. Later that day, Worrell had a team meeting and told his players that there would be no questioning of the umpire's decisions and no swearing on the field of play. The Australians and the umpires respected them for this and it helped to make the series a success.

Worrell united the West Indies in a way that no one else could have done. He had seen the bickering and parochialism of earlier tours and was determined that it would not happen again. His overriding aim was to make his players into a team in which talent could blossom. He did not want them to be merely a bunch of brilliant individuals.

The touring party recovered some of their confidence with victories over a Combined XI and Tasmania and then moved on to Sydney for the Third Test.

The West Indies scored 303 for 5 on the first day, thanks mainly to another wonderful unbeaten century from Garry Sobers. He was out soon on the second day and the West Indies collapsed to 339 all out. Davidson got five wickets and Benaud four. Australia reached 172 for 5 at the end of the day.

The next morning it was Australia's turn to collapse. Lance Gibbs, who had replaced Sonny Ramadhin in the side, took three wickets in four balls and they were all out for 202. With a healthy first innings lead of 137, the West Indies batted again but were soon in trouble at 22 for 3. Worrell played a captain's innings but was out just before the close for 82, the Windies finishing on 179 for 7.

Gerry Alexander had been 11 not out overnight and now picked an excellent time to score his first Test century (he also scored half centuries in all the other Test matches in the series). There was good support from Gibbs who batted for an hour and half for 18 before being stumped by Grout off Benaud. Hall, with uncharacteristic restraint, batted for over an hour for 24. Alexander was last out for a magnificent 108 and Australia were set 464 to win.

They started well and reached 182 for 2 by the close of play, with Neil Harvey on 84 not out and Norman O'Neill on 53 not out. The final day saw Australia succumb to the spin of Gibbs and Valentine on a turning pitch. At one point, Gibbs took four wickets for 2 runs and finished with 5 for 66. Valentine took four of the other wickets and Australia were all out for 241. The West Indies had squared the series.

The Fourth Test, played at Adelaide, was another extraordinary match. Kanhai scored a century and Worrell and Alexander both got half centuries in a first innings total of 393. Australia had reached 281 for 5 when Gibbs took a hat trick to make it 281 for 8. Then Des Hoare, playing in his only Test match, in place of the injured Davidson, helped Benaud to add 85 runs for the 9th wicket and Australia were all out for 366, just 27 runs short of the West Indies total.

In the second innings, Hunte scored 79 and Kanhai made another century. There were half centuries again for Worrell and Alexander. The West Indies declared on 432 for 6 leaving Australia an almost impossible target of 461. They finished the fourth day on 32 for 3 with defeat looking inevitable.

Despite some resistance from Norman O'Neill and Peter Burge, wickets fell at regular intervals. Australia were reduced to 207 for 9, with an hour and fifty minutes still to play, when Lindsay Kline came out to join Ken 'Slasher' Mackay. Almost immediately, Sobers, fielding close to the bat, appealed confidently for a catch from Mackay off Worrell's bowling. It was turned down and the two Australians embarked on one of greatest rearguard actions in Test history.

Although Mackay never scored a century in his thirty-seven Tests, he averaged just over 33 with the bat and scored 13 half centuries. The sobriquet of 'Slasher' was ironic. He was a very useful batsman especially in tight situations. Kline, on the other hand, never improved on his 15 not out that he made in this Test. Mackay, who had been dropped first ball, batted nearly four hours for his 62 not out. Amazingly, the pair held out till the close of play. The West Indies had missed out on a wonderful opportunity to take a winning lead in the series.

Australia only had a draw to play for on the last day so the match never acquired the legendary status of the 'Tied Test' where all four results were possible up to the last over. Nevertheless, it was yet another exciting game which left the series fascinatingly poised at 1 – 1 with one match to play.

The Australians had taken Worrell and his team to their hearts. After years of negative and tedious cricket, the Australian public was captivated by the series. Worrell and Benaud had promised to play positive cricket and they had remained true to their word. This is not the same thing as trying to hit every ball for six or always having three slips in place. Rather, it is having the philosophy of 'how can we win this game?' as opposed to 'how can we make sure we don't lose this game?'

The teams returned to Melbourne for the final Test. Benaud made the first positive move by winning the toss and putting the West Indies in to bat. The atmosphere was heavy and he probably expected the ball to move around more than it did. At the end of the day, Australia had the slight edge with the West Indies closing on 252 for 8. The next day was a Saturday and a world record crowd of 90,800 watched the game. A true testament to Worrell and his team.

Solomon and Hall had a 9th wicket partnership of 55 and the West Indies finished on 292. By the end of the second day, Australia had reached 236 for 3 and were very much in the driving seat. The West Indies fought back on the Monday with wickets for Sobers and Gibbs and Australia's first innings lead was restricted to 64. By the close of play, the Windies had reached 126 for 2, effectively 62 for 2 and everything still to play for.

All the top batsmen made starts but none could put together a big score. Worrell was cheered all the way to the wicket for what he knew would be his last Test innings in Australia. Sadly for him, and the West Indies, he only made 7. Gerry Alexander once again batted well and top scored with 73. He finished top of the batting averages for both sides and you would have got long odds on that at the start of the series. The West Indies were all out for 321 and so Australia needed 258 to win the game with a day and a bit to go. McDonald was out just before the end and Benaud went in as nightwatchman.

As discussed in Chapter 2, the concept of nightwatchman in cricket is a curious one. Does it really make sense to send in someone who isn't particularly good at batting when it's very important not to lose another wicket? It is interesting that Benaud took it upon himself, as captain, to undertake the duty. At least it is more logical for him to do the job, as he was a useful bat. Another example of his positive approach to the game.

As it happened he did not last long the next day but Simpson and O'Neill took the score on to 154 before Simpson was out 8 short of his century. With only another 104 runs needed, Australia were definitely favourites but wickets began to fall. As though to make up for his failure with the bat, Worrell proceeded to bowl 31 overs, concede only 43 runs and take 3 wickets. It was still anyone's game.

Australia edged closer and when Burge was the seventh wicket to fall, Australia needed just 8 runs to win. There was a moment of controversy when, with 4 runs needed, Grout late cut Valentine for two runs but the off bail had fallen to the ground. The umpires consulted and ruled that the batsman was not out and the runs should stand. Valentine then had Grout caught for no addition to the score. Another tied match was still a possibility, both sides could still win. Australia required 2 runs to win when Martin gave a chance which wasn't taken and they ran a single to bring the scores level. 'Slasher' Mackay had faced 51 balls for his 3 not out. He and Martin ran a bye and the Australians had won by 2 wickets.

The West Indies had lost the series but it didn't really matter. In truth, a drawn series, or even a West Indies win, would have been a fairer result. Both sides won one Test relatively comfortably. One Test, the West Indies should really have won and the other two Tests were very, very close.

Although it undoubtedly would have mattered to the West Indies players that they had lost the series, in the wider scheme of things they were still winners. They had played entertaining cricket throughout the tour. They had held their own with Australia. And last but not least, Frank Worrell had debunked the myth that a black man could not successfully captain the West Indies.

So captivated were the Australians with Worrell's leadership and charisma that they named the winners' trophy after the touring captain. Former Test player Ernie McCormick, a jeweller by profession, was commissioned to create a trophy incorporating the ball used in the Tied Test. Australia and the West Indies still play for the Frank Worrell Trophy today.[18]

Such was the appreciation of the West Indies touring party that the side was given a motorcade and tickertape farewell through the streets of Melbourne. Hundreds of thousands of people turned out to see them off. Melbourne came to a standstill. There has never been such a farewell for a visiting cricket team before or since. Frank Worrell and his team returned home from the tour as heroes.

---

18 Australia have held it since 1995 but the West Indies did hold it for seventeen years running before that. What goes around, comes around. In 2010, Pakistan beat Australia in a Test for the first time in fifteen years, so maybe it will be the West Indies turn again soon?

9. West Indies tour of England, 1963

In 1963, the Thames froze over, the Great Train Robbery took place, Kim Philby was named as the 'third man'[19], President Kennedy was assassinated, the Beatles had their first No.1 hit with *Please Please Me* and Frank Worrell brought his West Indian team to England.

Life was a lot simpler in 1963. For a start, there were only two TV channels, something that is more or less inconceivable to anyone brought up in today's multi-channel age. In the evening, the whole family would settle down and watch the *Dick Emery Show*. Later, if you were lucky, you might get a bit of Charlie Drake or Harry Worth. Ah, the good old days. Little wonder then that all cricket lovers looked forward to the West Indies tour of England with eager anticipation.

Apart from the West Indian cricket tour, the other major excitement in 1963 was the Profumo affair. It was a sensation that gripped the country for months and had repercussions well beyond the initial scandal. It had everything! Cabinet ministers, call girls, sex parties, Soviet spies, a socialite osteopath and a mysterious suicide.

John Profumo, educated at Harrow and Oxford, was the Secretary of State for War. He met Christine Keeler at Lord Astor's country mansion and they had a brief affair. Keeler, and

---

19 Not a cricket reference but Philby was a keen follower of the game. There couldn't have been much cricket for him to watch in Moscow; a high price to pay for betraying your country.

her friend, Mandy Rice-Davies, were 'associates' of Stephen Ward, a fashionable West End osteopath. His profession was probably quite useful bearing in mind the sort of parties he laid on for his friends and clients.

Profumo wasn't the first MP to have a fling with a 'call girl' and he surely won't be the last. Before the sixties, his affair would more than likely have remained simply as gossip for those in the know. However, by 1963, the world was changing and the media were not so deferential. Satirical magazines like *Private Eye* and TV programmes like *That Was The Week That Was* had a wonderful time.

With the rumours and speculation growing, Profumo made a big mistake. He lied to the House of Commons. In March 1963, he made a statement to the House saying that "no impropriety whatever" was involved in his relationship with Christine Keeler. Call me old-fashioned but it's hard to imagine a forty-eight-year-old government minister and a twenty-one-year-old 'call girl' having a relationship where there was no impropriety involved.

He might have got away with it but for the revelation that Keeler had also slept with Eugene Ivanov, a naval attaché at the Soviet embassy. The world was in the grip of the Cold War during the early sixties. The Bay of Pigs invasion and the Cuban missile crisis in 1962 had brought the world as close to a nuclear war as it has ever been.

The idea that the British Secretary of State for War was sleeping with the same woman as a Soviet naval attaché was too much for the FBI. They launched Operation Bowtie – possibly named after the only thing, apart from a mask that, allegedly, a naked Cabinet Minister was wearing when he served drinks at one of Stephen Ward's 'parties'. And he wasn't wearing it round his neck.

Harold Macmillan and John F. Kennedy were in the middle of delicate negotiations about the sale of Polaris missiles to the UK. The FBI feared that defence secrets had been compromised. To add a little spice to an already extremely hot story, the actor Douglas Fairbanks Jnr knew many of the people involved, including Ward and Keeler. He provided the FBI with regular reports of the various activities. It seems likely that he had a front row seat at some of Ward's parties and therefore was in a good position to let the FBI know what was going down, so to speak.

The game was up for Profumo. He had to apologise for lying to the House of Commons and resign from both the Government and his Parliamentary seat. The Establishment needed a scapegoat so they went for the easiest targets – Stephen Ward, Christine Keeler and Mandy Rice-Davies (proving that having a double-barrelled name was not enough to protect you from the English Establishment.)

In June 1963, Ward was charged with living off immoral earnings and procuring prostitutes. The case came to court the following month. The prosecuting counsel was Mervyn Griffith-Jones, who had been the prosecutor in the Lady Chatterley's Lover court case. He made a particularly harsh attack on Ward's character in his closing speech describing him as "a thoroughly filthy fellow" and "a wicked, wicked creature". Ward apparently took an overdose of sleeping tablets the following night and was discovered in a coma the next morning. The jury, with strong guidance from the judge, found Ward guilty of living off immoral earnings and he died three days later without regaining consciousness.

Ward had claimed that he was providing information to MI5 about Eugene Ivanov but they denied it at the time of his trial – well they would wouldn't they? Many years later, Ward's claim was corroborated by retired MI5 officers. Beyond doubt was the fact that Sir Roger Hollis, head of MI5, was a friend/client of his as was Sir Anthony Blunt, Surveyor of the Queen's Pictures. The latter was later exposed as the 'fourth man' in the Philby affair.

It was later established that Christine Keeler, Mandy Rice-Davies and others were pressured by the police to lie in court about their associations with Ward. It seems likely that Ward lent Keeler more money than she actually gave to him.

You may be thinking that this is all very interesting but what has it got to do with cricket. Well, as it happens, the Profumo affair made a major contribution in helping Britain get the only Prime Minister ever to have played first-class cricket.

The Tories had been in power since 1951 and Harold Macmillan had been Prime Minister since 1957. The Profumo Affair brought a huge amount of pressure on to the Tory party in general and Macmillan in particular. In October 1963, he resigned on the grounds of ill health. There were no elections for leaders in those days and the obvious successor was 'Rab' Butler, the 'unofficial' Deputy Prime Minister.

However, poor 'Rab' had not gone to Eton and was also considered a bit of a 'lefty' (these things are all relative). The 'magic circle' of Tory elders looked at all the likely candidates and decided that the job should go to the 14th Earl of Home. True, he was a member of the House of Lords at the time, not the House of Commons, but he had been educated at Eton and was damn good at cricket.

Using recent legislation that had enabled the 2nd Viscount Stansgate to become Anthony Wedgwood-Benn (or Tony Benn as we now know him), the 14th Earl of Home was transformed into plain old Sir Alec Douglas-Home. Macmillan advised the Queen to invite the Old Etonian to form a Government, presumably on the grounds that he was a jolly decent chap.

For a few weeks, Sir Alec Douglas-Home was Prime Minister without being a member of either the House of Lords or the House of Commons, a rather unusual state of affairs to say the least. He eventually got into the Commons through a by-election in the safe Tory seat of Kinross and West Perthshire. Willie Rushton, of *Private Eye* fame, stood against him but polled only 45 votes.

Sir Alec, or Lord Dunglass as he appeared in the scorebook, played ten first-class matches for six different teams including Middlesex, Oxford University, H.D.G. Leveson Gower's XI and the MCC (with whom he toured South America under Sir Pelham – aka Plum – Warner). Sadly, politics curtailed a promising cricketing career in 1927.

When Frank Worrell and his West Indies team arrived in April 1963, Macmillan was still PM and Gerry and the Pacemakers were top of the Hit Parade (that's what it was called then!) with '*How Do You Do It?*'. That was probably what the Gloucestershire team was asking Charlie Griffith as he took 8 for 23 when they were bowled out for just 60. The West Indies had also bowled out Worcestershire for 119 in the tour's opening first-class game. Worcestershire had Tom Graveney to thank for getting that many. He scored 75 of the runs himself. The tourists were looking very strong and the First Test was still a month away.

The match against Gloucestershire was noteworthy for Sir Learie Constantine's intervention in an ongoing dispute at a Bristol bus company which had refused to employ coloured workers.

Bristol in the early 1960s had around 3,000 residents of West Indian origin, some whom had served in the armed forces during the Second World War and others who had emigrated to Britain more recently. They suffered discrimination in housing and employment. One of their main grievances was with the Bristol Omnibus Company, which had been nationalised since 1950.

The company enforced a strict colour bar by refusing to employ blacks or Asians as bus crew. This was effectively endorsed by the Transport and General Workers' Union (TGWU). The company claimed white women would refuse to ride on buses driven by black men or would feel unsafe if they employed black bus conductors. It was an act of blatant racism and provoked Paul Stephenson, a twenty-six-year-old teacher and community officer working in St Pauls, an area of Bristol, to lead a boycott of the city's buses. His protest was backed by thousands of local people.

Tony Benn, a Bristol MP, lent his support and Sir Learie Constantine, who at the time was the High Commissioner for Trinidad and Tobago, wrote letters to the bus company condemning their actions. Sir Learie attended the tourist's game against Gloucestershire in early May and leaflets were handed out to West Indian players as they arrived at Bristol. Frank Worrell was unwilling to get embroiled in the situation. "We do not want to get involved in political matters," he said. Constantine's respect for Worrell was not diminished by his lack of involvement. They remained good friends to the end.

The protests and negotiations went on all summer. Sir Learie Constantine continued to be involved. On 28th August the company finally capitulated and agreed to lift the bar. It was the same day that Martin Luther King delivered his *I have a dream* speech.

It would take another five years before the Race Relations Act of 1968 made racial discrimination at the workplace illegal. The Bristol bus protest had played its part in bringing this about.

After Bristol, the West Indies moved on to Fenners and comfortably beat a Cambridge University side captained by Mike Brearley. The tourists scored 512, which included a ferocious maiden first-class century from Wes Hall in just sixty-five minutes.

In all, the Windies played ten first-class matches before the start of the First Test. This is in stark contrast with touring sides these days that seem to get off the plane, have a quick net, one knockabout match against a county side consisting of under-19s and Kolpak players and then go straight into a Test match. Back in 1963, the West Indies won 6 and drew 3 of their opening ten first-class matches.

The only game they lost was against Yorkshire. As was usually the way then, Yorkshire fielded a full strength side. Geoffrey Boycott, 'Best Young Cricketer of the Year' in 1963, couldn't even get in the team. Yorkshire made 226 in their first innings with Fred Trueman scoring 55. The West Indies were then bowled out for 109, Trueman taking 5 wickets. Opening for Yorkshire in the second innings, D.E.V. Padgett was hit in the face by a ball from Charlie Griffith and had to retire hurt. Brian Close declared at 145 for 6 and Yorkshire bowled the visitors out for 151 with Trueman again taking 5 wickets.

Clearly there was no thought of saving Trueman for the Test matches but perhaps there should have been. In the First Test at Old Trafford, the West Indies racked up 501 for 6 declared with Conrad Hunte scoring 182, Trueman taking 2 for 95 off forty overs. England made 205 and 296 and got hammered by 10 wickets.

Fiery Fred probably wasn't in the best of moods. He was due a £150 good conduct bonus from the recent winter tour of Australia. With the immaculate timing for which it was renowned in those days, the MCC had informed Trueman just before the Old Trafford Test that they were cutting £50 from it. The reduction was because of his alleged "behaviour off the field". Talking after lights out, walking with his hands in his pockets, not showing the Duke of Norfolk sufficient respect; that sort of thing. He threatened not to play for England again but eventually backed down.

The West Indies team that toured England in 1963 was well balanced and strong in all departments. Many of the players had experience of English conditions either from the last tour in 1957 or from playing in the Lancashire leagues. In the Test series, apart from Worrell with forty-five overs, all the bowling was done by four bowlers only – Hall, Griffith, Sobers and Gibbs. Ten players played in all five Tests and the only problem they had was with Conrad Hunte's opening partner. Carew, McMorris and Rodriguez were all tried with moderate success.

Hunte – the disciplined 'sheet anchor', restraining his natural aggression – and Kanhai – flamboyant, improvising and entertaining – were the batting stars in the Tests with Butcher and Sobers not far behind. Worrell scored an immaculate 74 not out at Old Trafford but after that did not get a big score in the Test matches. At the age of thirty-eight he was past his best but more than made up for it with his leadership and captaincy.

The West Indies emphatic win in the First Test put them in a confident mood. The previous year, the West Indies had beaten India 5 – 0 in the Caribbean so this was their sixth Test win in succession. After two one-day matches in Belfast and Dublin, they played Sussex at Hove. Ted Dexter – a 'scratch' golfer – was captain of Sussex as well as England and he must have wished he had opted for the golf course, as his county side collapsed for 59 in their first innings. The tourists declared at 287 for 9 with Sobers out one short of his 100. When Sussex batted again, Dexter made a century in two and a half hours but the West Indies went on to win the match with ease.

Dexter was an attractive and aggressive batsman and his hook rivalled that of Henry Cooper for effectiveness. On 18th June that year, at Wembley Stadium, a Cooper left hook knocked down Cassius Clay, as he was then known. Only the bell saved the future

Muhammad Ali from defeat. A mysterious split glove that needed fixing gave him the time to recover and he stopped Cooper with a cut eye in the next round.

The tourists moved on to Lords for the Second Test. Once again, just as in the tied Test at Brisbane, the West Indies were to be involved in an extraordinary match that set the series alight. Just as in Brisbane, all four results were possible at the start of the last over at the end of the final day.

Frank Worrell won the toss and batted. The game started in dramatic fashion with Hunte taking boundaries off the first three balls of Trueman's opening over. Thereafter runs dried up to such an extent that only 47 were scored by lunch. Derek Shackleton had been recalled to international duty at the age of thirty-eight, after a gap of more than eleven years. He replaced Brian Statham who had been disappointing at Old Trafford.

England had again gone into the match with two spinners – Allen and Titmus – but the latter didn't get a bowl in the first innings. The damp conditions favoured swing bowling and both Trueman and Shackleton used them well. The selectors were no doubt regretting that Statham was not playing instead of one of the spinners. At the close, the tourists were 245 for 6, Kanhai top scoring with 73. Honours were shared and the stage set for one of the most exciting games ever seen at Lords.

The West Indies were out for 301 on the morning of the second day, Fred Trueman taking 6 for 100 from his forty-four overs. Shackleton lacked the pace of Trueman but was very economical. He didn't take a wicket on the first day but ended the innings with three wickets in four balls. He finished with 3 for 93 off 50.2 overs. Not bad for an old timer!

John Edrich was out to the first ball he faced and Micky Stewart followed soon afterwards and England went into lunch at

20 for 2. In the afternoon, Dexter played one of his best innings for England, scoring 70 at nearly a run a ball. He took on the fast bowling of Hall and Griffith in imperious fashion, hooking, cutting and driving before Sobers trapped him LBW. Colin Cowdrey and Brian Close were out cheaply but Ken Barrington batted over three hours for 80.

The gates were closed well before play started on the Saturday and England managed to reach 297 mainly thanks to a fine innings of 52 not out from Fred Titmus. The West Indies lost early wickets and only an excellent innings from Butcher, supported by Worrell, kept them in the game. They finished the day in a good position on 214 for 5. After a rest day on Sunday, the tourists lost their advantage on Monday morning when five wickets went down for 15 runs in only six overs. Butcher was the ninth wicket having scored 133 out of a total of 229.

So England were set 234 to win. They were soon 31 for 3, but Barrington and Cowdrey came together and offered some resistance. They had to withstand a lot of short pitched bowling from Hall and Griffith and, with the score on 72, Cowdrey received a ball from Hall that broke the bone above his left wrist. He left the field to be replaced by Brian Close. When bad light stopped play at the end of the fourth day, England were 116 for 3 and the game was delicately poised.

Rain and bad light prevented play from starting until 2.20pm on the last day and, when they finally began, England struggled on a lively pitch. Barrington only added 5 to his overnight score and was out for 60. Jim Parks, who had replaced Keith Andrew in the team as wicket-keeper because of his superior batting, supported Close for a while, scoring 17, and at tea, England were 171 for 5. They needed 63 to win with 5 wickets left but one of those was Cowdrey in the dressing room with his fractured arm in a plaster.

After tea, the balance of the game swung back to the West Indians. First Parks was out, followed later by Titmus and Trueman who fell to successive balls. Brian Close had played an incredibly courageous, but mainly defensive, innings up to that point, taking numerous blows on the body and had the bruises afterwards to prove it! He had a similar experience in 1976 when he was recalled to the England team at the age of forty-five to face the fearsome West Indian pace attack. As a *Sky* commentator these days, Michael Holding, with his mellifluous and mellow tone, is always worth listening to. Watch his over to Close at Old Trafford in 1976 on *YouTube* and you see a different Holding. Seeing him deliberately bowl at Close's helmet-less head, at over 90 mph, is pretty scary even today.

Back at Lords in 1963, Close changed tactics and started to come down the pitch to Hall and Griffith to try and put them off their length. It worked for a while but then, with 15 runs needed, he edged to the keeper. With nineteen minutes to go, Derek Shackleton came out to join David Allen. Together they eked out a few runs and when the last over began, England needed 8 runs to win. The West Indies needed 2 wickets to win. The similarities with the tied Test in Brisbane extended to the fact that Wes Hall was to bowl the last over. Showing extraordinary stamina, he had managed to bowl for three hours and twenty minutes with only the tea interval as a break.

With encouraging words from Worrell, Hall began the final over of the match. Shackleton swung at the first ball and missed. He got a bat on the second ball and they ran a single. Allen turned the third ball to leg for a single. 3 balls to go. England needed 6 runs to win, the West Indies 2 wickets to win.

Hall charged in and bowled the fourth ball. Shackleton stumbled as he swung and missed. He looked up to see Allen running towards him. As Shackleton set off for the other end, Deryck Murray, the nineteen-year-old wicket-keeper, calmly threw the ball to Worrell. Not risking a throw at the stumps, the two thirty-eight-year-olds had a foot race which Worrell won by a couple of yards and Shackleton was run out.

This brought Cowdrey to the wicket with his left arm in plaster. Luckily the batsmen had crossed so Allen was facing. He had probably dreamt of this moment as all cricket loving schoolboys do. Two balls to go and the chance to hit a 6 to win the game for England. He played the fifth ball defensively back to the bowler. Hall went back to his mark. Whereas today there would be a cacophony of noise as the bowler ran in, according to Ian Woolridge writing for the *Daily Mail* at the time, there was "utter silence" as Hall ran in.

The ball was on target and heading for the middle stump. Allen played forward and met it with the middle of his bat. The match was a draw. It had captured the imagination of the country in a way that cricket games occasionally can. Such was the evenness of the contest that it would have been very hard on one side to lose. The West Indies were still 1 − 0 up in the series but they knew that they were in a battle.

It was straight down to Southampton for the West Indies after the match at Lords. They were scheduled to start against Hampshire the very next day. Understandably, Hall and Griffith were rested. It was a below par performance for the tourists with Gibbs and Valentine holding out on the last day for a draw.

Again with no rest day, the West Indies moved on to Southend to play Essex. They were probably glad of a break when rain delayed the start. Play started after tea with Trevor Bailey putting the visitors in on a lively pitch. It seemed a good decision when they were all out for 205 but when Essex batted, they were soon in trouble against Hall and Griffith. Only a brave and skilful innings of 29 from a nineteen-year-old Keith Fletcher prevented complete humiliation. As it was, Essex were all out for an embarrassing 56 with the follow-on being saved by one run. Fifties from McMorris and Hunte enabled the Windies to declare and at 92 for 4 in their second innings, rain saved Essex from probable defeat.

The next game in the Test series was at Birmingham. Gerry and the Pacemakers were No.1 again, this time with *I Like It*. At the start of 1963, the Beatles were not even the biggest band in Liverpool, Gerry and the Pacemakers were huge! The band's original name was Gerry Marsden and the Mars Bars but they had to change it when the Mars Company, producers of the infamous chocolate bar, complained! The Marianne Faithfull, allegedly apocryphal, anecdote would never have seemed quite the same if they had been able to keep the name.

Later in the year, Gerry and the Pacemakers were to have a third No.1, with a song that the Kop adopted as their own and is still sung at Anfield today. *You'll Never Walk Alone* was originally a show tune from the 1945 Rodgers and Hammerstein musical, *Carousel*. The Beatles also had three No.1s in the year and soon became the biggest band in the world but you can't see them perform now can you? Gerry and the Pacemakers, on the other hand, are still touring, presumably sponsored by their namesake.

In 1963 the music was still a bit saccharine. Apart from Gerry Marsden and his lot, Frank Ifield had two No.1s, Cliff Richard was going on a *Summer Holiday* and The Searchers were singing *Sweets For My Sweet*. It wasn't until the next year that the bands with a bit more edge came into their own. The Rolling Stones, The Animals and the Kinks all had their first No.1s in 1964.

As the two teams gathered at Edgbaston, the West Indians would have been feeling confident. They were one up in the series and most of their key players were in form. What they hadn't allowed for was the weather. A downpour had drenched the ground the day before the match was due to start. The slow pitch did not suit Hall and Griffith and it was the left arm swing of Sobers, bowling at a lively pace, which carried the greater threat. England finished the first day at 157 for 5 when rain prevented any further play after tea.

Most of the second day was lost to rain but there was time for England to be all out for 216 just before the close, Sobers taking 5 for 60 off thirty-one overs. On the third day, a Saturday as it always used to be in Tests, there was less than three hours play and the West Indies struggled to 110 for 4. Sunday being a rest day, the match resumed on Monday and the crowd were rewarded with a full day's play.

The West Indies were out for 186 with no player getting to fifty. Trueman reduced his pace and, cutting the ball both ways, again got five wickets. He was well supported by the medium pace of Dexter who claimed four of the other wickets.

England steadily built on their first innings lead when they batted a second time. Phil Sharpe of Yorkshire, a brilliant slip fielder, was the replacement for the injured Colin Cowdrey. He came in at No.6 and batted fluently with Dexter initially, then Tony Lock. When Lock, who had come in for Allen, was out for 56 on the morning of the last day, Dexter declared. Sharpe, on début, had scored 85 not out.

The stage was set for an exciting finish. The West Indies had to make 309 in just under five hours. With the stroke makers they had in their side, this was definitely possible, but it was not to be. They were 55 for 3 at lunch and then collapsed to 91 all out. Trueman took the last six wickets to fall at the cost of four runs. He finished with twelve wickets in the match for 119 runs, the best

Test analysis of his whole career. This was done at the grand old age, for a fast bowler, of thirty-two.

The tourists had four games to recover their winning ways before the next Test. Rain ensured that their two-day game at Sunderland against the Minor Counties was a draw. The team contained G. Boycott (Yorkshire) batting at No.4. Yorkshire? A Minor County? Surely not? The other players were all representing counties like Cheshire, Oxfordshire and Wiltshire. I'm not sure what Boycott was doing there. Maybe he just turned up and asked for a game? Occasional bowler Seymour Nurse bowled him for 16, so he wouldn't have been very happy.

The next match also contained an oddity: H.D. Bird opening for Leicestershire and being cleaned bowled by Garry Sobers in both innings. Dickie Bird, born in Barnsley, famously played club cricket in the same team as Geoffrey Boycott and Michael Parkinson. He played for Yorkshire between 1956 and 1959 but could not command a regular place at a time when the county was particularly strong. Dickie scored 181 not out against Glamorgan in 1959 and was dropped for the next match when players returned from the Test side. He joined Leicestershire the next season but always regretted leaving Yorkshire. As an umpire he was idiosyncratic, to say the least, and somewhat eccentric. He once arrived at the Oval five hours early because the Queen was due to attend the Test match. You can't help thinking that one of his relatives emigrated to New Zealand some time in the past, got married and Billy Bowden was the result. However, Dickie Bird had the respect of the players because he kept his sense of humour and, crucially, got most of his decisions right.

The West Indies went on to beat Derbyshire and Middlesex comfortably before arriving at Leeds for the Fourth Test. The tourists had not played well in the damp conditions at Edgbaston.

Although most of the team were used to wet English summers it didn't mean they enjoyed them. The good news for the tourists was that first of all the sun came out at Headingley and then Worrell won the toss.

The West Indies chose to bat and lost three early wickets, but Sobers and Kanhai came together and put on 143 runs. Garry Sobers went on to his century and the visitors finished on a total of 397. The pace of Griffith soon had England in trouble and eight wickets went down for only 93. Tony Lock again got a fifty and, helped by Fred Titmus, managed to get the total to 174.

Worried that the pitch would deteriorate, Worrell did not enforce the follow-on. Although Hunte and McMorris were out cheaply, Kanhai and Butcher piled on the runs. Sobers scored 52 in quick time and the West Indies were all out for 229, scored in three and a half hours.

England were faced with the prospect of having to score 453 on a pitch helping the bowlers. Things did not start well when Sobers, opening instead of Hall, bowled Stewart in his first over. There was some resistance from Ken Barrington and also Brian Bolus playing in his first Test but both were out before the close.

The next day, Close and Parks scored aggressive fifties but England were all out for 231, with the wickets shared between Sobers, Griffith and Gibbs. The West Indies were 2 – 1 up in the series with one to play.

After draws against Surrey, again, and Glamorgan, followed by a win against Warwickshire, the West Indies had a chance for revenge against Yorkshire who had beaten them at Middlesborough in May. A green pitch tempted Hunte to put the opposition in. The first three batsmen – all young uncapped players – must have made him think he had made the wrong decision. John Hampshire (who later scored a century for England on début against the West

Indies in 1969), Geoffrey Boycott (back from the Minor Counties) and Richard Hutton (son of Sir Len) took the score to 150 for 1.

The more experienced players all failed until a dashing 50 from Don Wilson, Yorkshire's left arm spinner, helped the county to a total of 260. When the visitors batted, Rodriguez scored an impressive 93 which secured him a place in the final Test. Nurse hit 77 and then Sobers stroked a brilliant 100 in under three hours.

Hunte declared with a lead of 98 and would have expected to get another chance for some more batting practice. He wasn't needed. Yorkshire were all out for 96 with Griffith taking 5 for 12 off ten overs. Sweet revenge for the West Indies against the only county side to beat them all tour.

Northamptonshire had the better of the next match, with Colin Milburn scoring a magnificent 100 in the first innings and an exhilarating 88 in the second. 'Ollie' Milburn was a huge talent in every sense, his size making Samit Patel seem positively anorexic. He was talked about as a possible England player in 1963 but didn't get picked until 1966, when the West Indians were visiting again. Apart from his weight, his 'larger than life' character and gregarious nature probably didn't do him any favours in the eyes of the selectors. Considering he only played nine Test matches, he is remembered with great affection by a great many people. His contentious exclusion from the England party to visit South Africa in 1968 was completely overshadowed by the Basil D'Oliveira affair.

In 1963, after the first two days play, Northants were strong favourites to win the game against the West Indies but rain washed out the last day of the match and it ended in a draw. The final outing before the Fifth Test was another draw, this time against Nottinghamshire and then it was off to the Oval for the game that would decide the outcome of the series.

Only four players for England – Dexter, Close, Barrington and Trueman – played in all five Tests. This compares to ten players who played in all the Tests for the West Indies. Assuming a team is playing well, to have a settled side is a definite advantage. The players get used to one another and camaraderie is built up. The captain knows what he can get from each member of the team. Most importantly for the 1963 tourists, Worrell knew how to get the best out of Hall and Griffith.

Fast bowlers are notoriously difficult to handle at any level of cricket. As a general rule, the faster the bowler the more temperamental the player. Trueman certainly fitted this stereotype but his partner Brian Statham was the exception that proved the rule. Nicknamed 'Gentleman George' (in stark contrast to his fellow pacemen, 'Fiery Fred' and 'Typhoon Tyson'); he had to be persuaded to bowl a bouncer. Frank Tyson told the story of a West Indian bowler who hit Jim Laker over the eye in a Test match during the 1950s. When the offender came out to bat, Statham was encouraged to reciprocate with a bouncer. He replied: "No, I think I'll just bowl him out."

Statham was recalled for the final Test at the Oval, joining Trueman and Shackleton in a three-man pace attack. Statham was a class act and still stands fifth in the all time England wicket taking list with 252 wickets. Despite the plethora of Test matches in the last twenty years, no bowler has yet overtaken Botham, Willis, Trueman, Underwood and Statham in the England list. Brian Statham was quicker than Shackleton and invariably just as accurate. The West Indies were going to have to fight hard for their runs.

Dexter won the toss and chose to bat so Hall and Griffith had the first chance to make their mark, literally in the case of Wes Hall. He hit John Edrich early on and then, in the sixth over, sent down two successive bouncers at Brian Bolus. The umpire, Syd Buller warned Worrell about excessive short pitched bowling. Towards the end of the day, he warned Griffith directly, under the 'Fair and Unfair play' law. Unlike his umpiring colleagues in 1984, Buller at least had the courage to try to implement the spirit and the law of cricket but by then the damage to England's batting line up had been done. They collapsed from 216 for 4 to 275 all out. Phil Sharpe top scored with 63 and Griffith took six wickets.

The West Indies began their innings the next day and having reached the safety of 184 for 3, they too collapsed to 246 all out. Conrad Hunte contributed a disciplined 80. Frank Worrell, given a standing ovation as he went out for his last ever Test innings, was bowled by Statham for just 9.

So the home side had the slight advantage at the halfway stage. In the second innings, their fragile top order succumbed again. Sharpe batted for over three hours making 83 but the next best score was Barrington with 28. Sobers bowled superbly taking 3 for 77 from thirty-three overs. Griffith also got 3 wickets, Hall cleaned up the tail and England were all out for 223.

The series had been hard fought. Only in the third Test had the West Indies been outplayed. Now they needed to score 253 in the last innings to clinch the series. The tourists had collapsed at Edgbaston chasing 309. Would they do so again? They negotiated the last few overs of the third day safely and finished on 5 for 0 at the close of play.

The gates were closed early on Monday, 26th August. Over 25,000 spectators were in the ground, nearly two thirds were West Indian supporters. These days, tickets are purchased in advance, on line, with credit cards and cost around £100, so the scene at the Oval in 1963 would no longer be possible. The exuberance of their supporters must have helped to inspire the West Indies team and certainly added to the sense of occasion.

The visitors had a stroke of good fortune in their quest for victory. Trueman had injured his ankle on Saturday and, despite treatment over the weekend, he was unable to bowl on the last day. This gave the West Indies a huge boost. With 34 wickets, Trueman was far and away England's leading wicket taker in the series. Shackleton came next with 15.

Hunte and Rodriguez gave the tourists a solid start with an opening partnership of 78. Then Kanhai came in and scored a sparkling 77 at more than a run a minute. Finally, with a jubilant crowd getting ever closer to the boundary ropes, Butcher and Hunte saw their side home. The West Indies had won the match by 8 wickets and Hunte finished on 108 not out. Hundreds of spectators invaded the pitch to celebrate the victory.

The West Indies had deservedly taken the newly established Wisden Trophy, three games to one. Griffith almost matched Trueman by taking 32 wickets and he had great support from Sobers, Gibbs and Hall. There was, however, a significant difference in the batting with no England player scoring a century in the series whereas there were four centuries for the West Indies – two for Hunte, one for Sobers and one for Butcher. Kanhai didn't get a century but had a wonderful series finishing as the leading run scorer with 497 runs.

It was a fitting end to Frank Worrell's Test career. His aim had been to establish the West Indies as a serious international force. The epic series in Australia followed by the 5 – 0 home triumph against India and the series win in England had unequivocally done that.

By the time the tourists went home to the Caribbean in the middle of September, they had played thirty-eight games in all, including thirty first-class matches. Apart from the defeat to England at Edgbaston and Yorkshire's victory in May, the only other match the West Indies lost was a one-day Challenge match against Sussex, the Knockout Cup winners.

Lord Ted had got some compensation for losing the Test series, by leading Sussex to victory in the first Knockout Competition Final at Lords. Although Gillette were involved as low key sponsors it wasn't until the following year that it became known as the Gillette Cup. It seems strange now, some counties were lukewarm about sponsorship and one day cricket. Nowadays you have only got to say 'Charles Colville' and a county will put on a one-day match at the drop of a hat.

One-day cricket continued to grow in popularity throughout the sixties but it was the 1971 Gillette Cup semi-final between Lancashire and Gloucestershire that really established the game in the public's cricket consciousness. The 60-over-a-side match was watched by a full house at Old Trafford. Rain delayed the finish until nearly 9 o'clock in the evening when, in the gathering gloom, David Hughes became a Lancashire folk hero by hitting 24 runs from a John Mortimer over.

These days, umpires seem to take players off for bad light at the slightest opportunity. Back in 1971 the attitude was a little more relaxed. Jack Bond, the ultimately victorious Lancashire captain, had earlier asked Arthur Jepson, one of the umpires, about the bad light. "What's that up there?" asked Jepson, pointing to the sky. "The moon," replied Bond. "Well how far do you want to see?" said Arthur.

The West Indies were to become the kings of one day cricket in the 1970s, but in 1963 they were still getting to grips with the new form of the game. Put in by Dexter at Hove, they soon found themselves four wickets down for just nine runs. A brilliant partnership of 104 in only an hour between Sobers and Butcher rescued the tourists but they were all out for 177, with eight of their allocated 55 overs unused. Sussex got home with three overs to spare and, showing how expectations have changed over the years, *Wisden* describes their reply as "managing to score at a brisk rate".

The tour ended with a light-hearted charity match against Sir Learie Constantine's XI at the Oval. His team included Len Hutton, Godfrey Evans and Alec Bedser. Over 600 runs were scored on the day and Frank Worrell, playing his last innings in England, top scored for the West Indies with 68.

The tour had been an undoubted success. Increased immigration from the West Indies during the 50s and early 60s meant that the tourists received plenty of support in the major conurbations. Such was the popularity of the tourists that their next visit to England was brought forward to 1966. Until that time there had typically been six years between tours. Four of *Wisden's* 1963 'Cricketers of the Year' were West Indians – Sobers, Hunte, Kanhai and Griffith. There was recognition for Frank Worrell too when he was knighted in the 1964 New Year's Honours.

Garry Sobers had an outstanding tour. He played in twenty-four of the first-class matches, scoring more runs and bowling more overs than any other player. He also took 29 catches for good measure. Sobers was Worrell's natural successor and he was to lead the West Indies to victory when they returned in 1966.

10. England tour of Australia, 1928/29

The Holy Grail for Test batsmen is to end their career with a batting average of over 60. Only four players have achieved this: Don Bradman, Graeme Pollock, George Headley and Herbert Sutcliffe.

The rest of the top ten is made up of the following who didn't quite reach 60. Eddie Paynter, Ken Barrington, Everton Weekes, Walter Hammond, Garry Sobers and Jack Hobbs. No modern players feature in the top ten of Test averages. Garry Sobers is the most recent and he played his last Test in 1973.

The best current batsmen – Ponting, Tendulkar, Sangakkara and Kallis – are all in the mid 50s and unlikely to make the 60 benchmark. Relatively recent players who you might think would have qualified – Lara, Richards, Gavaskar and Miandad – all have Test averages in the early 50s.

It goes without saying that averages are not everything. Ian Botham averaged just over thirty-three in Test matches but his batting stopped the traffic and won games for England. Jonathan Trott will probably finish his Test career with a higher batting average than Ian Bell but who would you rather watch bat?

Four players who are in the top ten were involved in England's tour to Australia in 1928/29. This tour doesn't seem to get mentioned much, which is a shame because England stuffed the Australians 4 – 1. Maybe it's because the 'Bodyline' tour that followed it in 1932/33 is referred to interminably. England stuffed the Australians 4 − 1 in that one too!

The four players involved in the games on the 1928/29 tour were Jack Hobbs, who was still opening for England along with Herbert Sutcliffe, the consummate professional from Yorkshire. A young Don Bradman was playing for Australia but he was dropped after the first Test. Walter Hammond, making his first tour of Australia, made up the quartet of top ten players.

Wally Hammond was a complex, enigmatic man. He does not always get the recognition that his talents and achievements deserve. For a while in the 1930s, only Bradman challenged him for the title of 'greatest batsman on the planet.' Some claimed he was better than Bradman. Certainly Len Hutton, who did not give praise lightly, said: "I preferred to see an hour of Walter Hammond to eight or ten hours of Don Bradman."

Hammond had poise and style in abundance. Whereas Bradman is often referred to, perhaps a touch unfairly, as a 'run machine', Hammond's power, class and elegance at the crease are invariably the features that writers highlight. Neville Cardus was a fan from the first moment he saw him. He witnessed his 250 against Lancashire in 1925 and wrote: "To be present at the rise of a star in the sky and to know it is going to be glorious − here is a moment thrilling indeed to men who live their lives imaginatively." Classic Cardus hyperbole but you get the point.

Hammond dominated English cricket during the ten years leading up to the Second World War. He was top of the national batting averages for every year from 1933 until the outbreak of war, and then again in 1946. He played in eighty-five Tests, captaining England before the war and immediately after it. He was reluctant to turn his arm over but when he did bowl he could be devastating. He generally bowled medium quick but could be genuinely fast if he put his mind to it. In his early days, he was an outstanding cover point fielder. Later he moved to slip where he was considered to be the best in the game. Had he bowled more, he would have undoubtedly rivalled Sobers as the best all-rounder ever seen in the game.

County and Test colleagues often described him as moody, introverted and distant, and those were some of the nice things they said about him. He was reluctant to give praise and rarely encouraged the younger players. Despite his great talent he often seemed unsure of himself. At the root of his insecurity was an uncertainty of his social status; never really at ease with his fellow professionals nor completely comfortable with the amateurs he later joined.

He was certainly a very private man and he probably had quite a lot to be private about. Eddie Paynter was asked for his enduring memory of the Test colleague that he had played and toured with. Maybe his exquisite cover drive or an outstanding slip catch or beating the Australians? The Lancastrian replied, "Wally, well, yes – he liked a shag!" Hammond, although shy, was a ladies man. He was very attractive to women and he in turn was rather partial to them.

His womanising, both before and during his first marriage, does not explain why so many of his fellow players did not get on with him. There would be a lot of unpopular players if that was the case. To most of his teammates he was a remote, seemingly lonely figure. They admired his cricketing prowess without question but few got close to him.

Hammond was an only child. He was born in Dover but spent most of his childhood in Hong Kong and Malta where his father was stationed in the army. Commissioned during the First World War, his father was killed in action in 1918. By this time, Walter

168

was boarding at Cirencester Grammar School in Gloucestershire. Success playing local cricket for Cirencester got him a county trial and, securing his mother's approval, he signed as a professional for Gloucestershire straight from school in August 1920.

Grace, Hobbs and Hammond were the three truly great English batsmen. It is coincidental that two of them – Grace and Hammond – played for Gloucestershire but this nearly didn't happen. After a few modest appearances at the end of the 1920 season and even less success in 1921, Hammond began to find his feet early in the 1922 season, only to fall foul of Lord Harris, Hon. Treasurer and omnipresent influence at the MCC.

Lord Harris, who once sacked an umpire for mistakenly giving a young Gubby Allen out LBW in a Gentlemen versus Players match at Lords, had been a dominant presence at the MCC for fifty years. He found out that although Hammond had been educated and brought up in Gloucestershire, he did not actually have a home there as his mother was living in Hampshire. Lord Harris, who incidentally was affiliated to Kent, decreed that Hammond did not qualify for Gloucestershire under the residency rules.[20] Harris saw himself as a bastion against anarchy and Bolshevism infiltrating cricket. Hammond could of course play for Kent if he wished, since he had been born in Dover.

Gloucestershire hung on to Hammond but he had to miss the rest of the 1922 season in order to qualify for them. Lord Harris was an autocratic ass, full of his own self-importance. Like so many people in power, a stickler for the rules when it suited him.

---

20 Also in 1922, the Kent Committee led by Harris queried the right of Alfred Jeacocke, a leading amateur of the day, to play for Surrey. They claimed his house was in Kent and only the other half of the street was in Surrey. Jeacocke had to stop playing while the MCC investigated. He only resumed playing for Surrey the following season.

The writer Benny Green describes him thus: "a bigot who always protested his own rectitude with absolute sincerity." In 1896 Harris, then President of the MCC, had barred Ranjitsinhji from playing for England against Australia at Lords on the grounds that he had been born in India. Lord Harris himself had been born in Trinidad but that had not stopped him turning out for England four times, captaining on each occasion. He had been school captain of the Eton XI so he was well qualified.

Benny Green's memorable description of Lord Harris continues: "He appears to have been a sort of moral imbecile who took up a succession of bogus ethical positions without ever perceiving the faintest trace of self-delusion."

Following the Hammond incident, Harris had a famous exchange in the Long Room at Lords with Lord Dearhurst, the president of Worcestershire. There was no love lost between the two of them, as illustrated by Lord Dearhurst's greeting. "Good morning my Lord. How many more young cricketers' careers have you buggered up this year?"

Walter Hammond showed great promise in his first three seasons for Gloucestershire but without the consistency that came as he matured. Jack Hobbs put him at the top of his list of future England players. He wrote in 1925 that Hammond was "potentially a very great all-rounder." This was before his 250 against Lancashire when Hammond took apart the Australian Ted McDonald, at the time the fastest bowler playing in England.

His obvious potential, coupled with the occasional devastating performance like the one at Old Trafford, got him selected for the MCC tour of the West Indies. The tour started well for Hammond when he scored 238 not out in a representative game against the West Indies who were not yet a full Test side. It ended disastrously.

Hammond became ill in British Guiana. He scored a century there and even bowled twenty-five overs in the next game at Jamaica but the infection he had picked up grew worse. He was in tremendous pain and discomfort on the journey home. The nature of the illness was never fully explained. A mosquito bite in the groin area was identified as a possible cause. He had to be carried off the ship on its return to England and taken straight to hospital.

It is no exaggeration to say that he very nearly died. In the days before antibiotics, blood infections were very hard to treat. At one point, the surgeons contemplated amputation of his leg but thankfully his mother refused to allow it. Only his physical strength and robust constitution saw him through. He was in a nursing home for months. The doctors did not really know how to deal with the illness. Often the treatment made things worse. He literally did not have the strength to get up and take another shot.

Hammond survived but missed the whole of the 1926 cricket season. Pelham 'Plum' Warner, chairman of the England selectors and the man who took over from Lord Harris as the main influence in the MCC, came to visit him. He had been an admirer of Hammond from the early days and his reassurance and support meant a lot to the twenty-three old. Hammond later wrote that Warner's visit "gave me the strength to turn the dark corner from hopelessness back to life."

Hammond and Warner were to become good friends despite their age difference and gap in social class. Warner was influential in persuading Hammond later to become an amateur and subsequently captain of England.

Gloucestershire arranged for him to spend the winter of 1926/27 in South Africa to continue his convalescence. He played some club cricket, swam every day, enjoyed the sunshine and gradually got his strength back. It paid off handsomely. Hammond had an outstanding season in 1927 scoring nearly 3,000 runs at an average of 69.

Once again he delivered the goods for Gloucestershire at Old Trafford. He was out for 99 in the first innings "being careless" as he wrote later. Then in the second innings he hooked and drove McDonald to distraction. Cardus described his knock of 187 in the *Manchester Guardian*:

> "It was one of the greatest innings ever witnessed on the ground. No other living Englishman could have given us cricket so full of mingled style and power, an innings of strength, bravery, sweetness and light. Not an ounce of power seemed to go to waste. Art directed the driving force of it all."

Already a fan, Cardus was now a lifelong convert. Hammond had still not played a Test match nor did he get the chance that season. New Zealand were visiting but they had not yet attained Test status. During the 1927 season, Hammond scored 1,000 runs before the end of May, only the third player to achieve this feat at the time. W.G. Grace in 1895 and Tom Hayward in 1900 being the others.

Wally Hammond made his Test début in South Africa the following winter. He had only modest success in the three Test series. Back in England for the 1928 season, Hammond once again had a very productive summer. At the Cheltenham Festival, he scored a century in each innings against Surrey and took ten catches in the match, still a first-class record for a fielder other than a wicket-keeper. His total of 78 catches that season is also still a world record and, with the onset of one day cricket, likely to remain so for evermore.

Hammond followed the Surrey match with 9 for 23 against Worcestershire, scored 80 when Gloucestershire batted and then got another 6 wickets in the second innings to help his side to victory without needing to bat again. He finished the season with 2,825 runs at an average of nearly 66 and 84 wickets at an average of 23. As well as helping his county to fifth place in the championship, he also played in three Test matches against the West Indies that summer. There were no centuries for Hammond but he had done enough to be on the boat when it left for Australia in September.

Only seven players have scored more than 50,000 runs in first-class cricket and five of them were in England's team for the First Test which started at Brisbane on 30th November, 1928. Hobbs and Sutcliffe opened. Phil Mead of Hampshire came in at number 3, followed by Hammond. Patsy Hendren of Middlesex, batting at six, was the fifth member of that exclusive club.

So there were plenty of contenders to be the batting star of the English team. Jack Hobbs, the Master, was making his last tour of Australia. Herbert Sutcliffe, brought up in Pudsey, the same Yorkshire town as Len Hutton, was vastly experienced. As he happily admitted himself, he was not as stylish a player as Hobbs but he fought off strong opposition to become his England opening partner for many years. His fellow Yorkshire opener Percy Holmes was one of the unlucky ones, only playing for his country seven times. Holmes had an outstanding county career which included the famous opening partnership with Sutcliffe of 555 against Essex.

Phil Mead started playing for Hampshire in 1905. Despite being one of the most consistent batsmen in the country for twenty years, he had few opportunities to play for England because of the remarkable strength of batting during that time. As well as the competition from Hobbs, Sutcliffe and Hendren, Mead's career more or less paralleled that of Frank Woolley. The stylish Kent all-rounder – another member of the 50,000 runs club, along with W.G. Grace – played sixty-four Tests compared with Mead's seventeen.

When C.P. (Phil) Mead arrived in Australia in 1928 at the age of forty-one, he was greeted by a local official who claimed to have watched Mead's 'father' play for England in 1911. The amused Mead had to inform him that in fact it was he himself who had, seventeen years earlier, made his first trip to Australia.

Mead was not the most graceful player but quick on his feet and very difficult to get out. The writer, R.C. Robertson-Glasgow, who often played against him, wrote that Mead "pervaded a cricket pitch .... occupied it and encamped on it! His bat always appeared wider than others."

Before every ball Phil Mead received he would turn to square leg, touch his cap peak four times, then tap his bat four times at the crease before taking four small shuffling steps forward. He would no doubt be delighted to know that he is fourth in the all time run makers table with 55,061 runs and no chance of anyone ever overtaking him. If an impatient bowler attempted to bowl before he had completed his ritual, he simply held up his hand, stopped him in his run up and went through the whole performance again. Jonathan Trott, eat your heart out!

Only Jack Hobbs scored more than Patsy Hendren's 170 first-class centuries and only Hobbs and Woolley improved on his career aggregate of 57,611 runs. He was an exciting aggressive batsman, fearless against fast bowling. Hendren was similar in style to Denis Compton who joined him in the Middlesex side in 1937 at the end of Hendren's career. True to his Irish ancestry, he was the life and soul of any touring party. He was an entertaining player and a humorous companion who helped make the 1928/29 tour of Australia a happy and successful one

With Douglas Jardine also in the side, which was led by the dashing bon viveur Percy Chapman, there was a lot of batting competition for the twenty-five year old Walter Hammond making his first tour of Australia. Chapman, an amateur of course, was a popular captain. There was harmony within the England camp both on and off the field. Chapman was an inspirational fielder and hard-hitting middle-order batsman. Amateurs and professionals mixed as equals in his team – not always the case at country or county level. Fun was had by all off the field, as well as hard endeavour on it (although it is unlikely that Jardine would have admitted to having fun in Australia.) It helped of course that most of the games were won.

The games in that Test series were 'timeless' matches. This must be one of the reasons why so many players from before the Second World War have higher Test batting averages than their modern day equivalents. There was much less pressure on batsmen to move the score along. Other reasons could be the attacking fields that were set and often kept in place for most of the day. If you were good enough to survive as a batsman you got good value for your shots. In addition, although there were some exceptional fielders at the time, the overall standard of fielding was not as high as it is today. Fast bowlers did not feel so inclined to throw themselves around trying to save runs. However, set against these advantages, pre Second World War batsmen had to cope with uncovered pitches and there were no games against any 'weaker' Test nations.

England only needed five days to beat Australia in the First Test at Brisbane. They scored 521 in the first innings, Patsy Hendren top scoring with 169 and Harold Larwood rather surprisingly next best with 70. Larwood went on to take 6 for 32, the best figures of his Test career, as the Australians were bowled out for 122. Chapman did not enforce the follow-on and England reached 342 for 8 on the fourth day when he declared.

This was the first ever declaration in a Test in Australia, with 'timeless' matches there was little incentive to do so, but Chapman probably thought his team could defend a lead of 741. He was right. With two of the team unable to bat – Kelleway had food poisoning and Gregory a knee injury – Australia were shot out for only 66.

Don Bradman, playing in his first Test, scored 18 and 1 and was dropped for the next match. Phil Mead top scored in England's second innings with 73 but was also dropped and George Geary, a bowler, brought in for the rest of the series. Wally Hammond made a limited contribution with the bat and got no wickets but he kept his place.

The next Test was played at Sydney. Jack Hobbs celebrated his forty-sixth birthday during the game. He was presented with a 'shilling fund' collection organised by an Australian newspaper and escorted round the ground to the acclaim of the 58,000 crowd. This is surely a tradition that should be revived. For instance, Alastair Cook's birthday is on Christmas Day (insert your own joke here about being England's saviour). What a nice touch it would be to give the occupants of the Hill (now redeveloped and called the Victor Trumper Stand) an opportunity to show their appreciation of Cook's talents.

At the Second Test in 1928, Wally Hammond must have thought it was his birthday too. He scored a majestic 251 out of England's total of 636. This remained England's highest ever total in Australia until the 644 in the 2011 Test at Sydney. It was Hammond's first century for his country. The *Sydney Morning*

Herald (an Australian newspaper please note) declared that "figures cannot convey the charm and variety of his strokes. It is doubtful if there is a player in the world from whom the ball travels with more pace."

Hammond had transformed himself from a free-flowing, stylish and sometimes impulsive batsman into a more responsible, balanced and mature player. He cut out the hook completely because of the risk inherent in the shot. He still attacked the bowling but his shots were predominantly drives in the V between mid-wicket and cover point. He was so powerful and such a perfect timer of the ball that he was able to score prodigiously despite limiting his range of strokes.

George Geary had earlier justified his inclusion in the team by taking 5 for 35 and helped to bowl out Australia for 253 in their first innings. When they batted again, Woodfull and Hendry both scored centuries and put on 215 for the second wicket but Australia were eventually all out for 397. Percy Chapman reversed the batting order and England lost 2 wickets getting the 15 runs they needed to win. This could not disguise the fact that Australia had been hammered once again and England were two up in the series.

Ponsford had retired hurt when hit by a rising ball from Larwood in the Second Test and Bradman had come on as a sub to field in his place. For the Third Test at Melbourne, Bradman was back in the side. He scored 79 out of a total of 397 when Australia won the toss and batted first.

The Hammond/Bradman rivalry was at a very nascent stage but Wally Hammond made sure he stayed well ahead on points by scoring another double hundred when England batted. He scored exactly 200 out of a total of 417.

His performance in the previous Test at Sydney had earned him a 'shilling fund' collection organised by the *Sydney Sun*. As a young professional, Hammond would have been glad of the money. Now the Australian newspapers were getting concerned that such a relatively inexperienced batsman was dominating their bowling so easily.

Not to be outdone, Bradman scored a century in the Australian second innings total of 351 but England won the match when they reached 332 for 7. Herbert Sutcliffe took the honours for England with a century; Hammond was run out for 32. The 'timeless match' format benefited England as, this time, the game lasted into the seventh day.

The tourists now had an unassailable 3 – 0 lead and had retained the Ashes. Wally Hammond had established himself as a star in the eyes of the Australian public. Cricket spectators were not quite so partisan in those days. They obviously wanted their team to win but were more likely than today's supporters to appreciate high-quality play whoever produced it.

Ideally of course, the Australian crowd wanted a hero of their own and in the next Test they got one. The Fourth Test at Adelaide saw the most exciting game in the series. In this match, Australia found their batting star, but it wasn't Bradman .... yet. Nineteen-year-old Archie Jackson scored 164 on his Test début. His elegant composure and creative stroke play marked him out for greatness. Born in Scotland and brought to Australia as a child, Jackson had a delicate physique and poor health. He played in only eight Test matches and died of tuberculosis at the age of twenty-three. He was a truly gifted player and those who saw him bat were convinced of his potential to be one of the greats.

Hammond once again was England's champion, scoring a century in both innings. Australia more or less gave up trying to get him out and instead concentrated on restricting his run scoring and getting at the other batsmen. Hammond's second innings of 177 was a masterpiece and set up the exciting finish. The only other contributions of note were Douglas Jardine with 98 and Maurice Tate a quick fire 47. Australia needed 348 to win and could take as long as they liked to get them.

In the first innings, Jackson had lost his opening partner Woodfull for 1, then Hendry had gone for 2 and finally Kippax for just 3 runs. To lose three experienced players with only 19 runs on the board, made his innings of 164 even more remarkable. The second time around, Jackson and Woodfull put on 65 in just under two hours before the young débutant was caught behind for 36.

The Australian innings progressed steadily and at 320 for 7, with Bradman at the wicket and only 28 needed, they were favourites to win. Then Oldfield played the ball to Jack Hobbs in the covers and called Bradman for a run. Maybe Oldfield thought that the forty-six-year-old Hobbs would be tired after seven days of play? Maybe later in his career, Bradman would have sent Oldfield back? As it was, Bradman responded and was run out by an accurate throw from Hobbs.

It was the deciding moment of the match. Jack 'Farmer' White,[21] the slow left-armer from Somerset, went on to get the next two wickets to add to the six he already had in the innings and England won by 12 runs. White bowled 124.5 overs in the game and took a total of thirteen wickets. England were 4 – 0 up and Hammond had scored 779 runs in five successive innings. In the Fourth Test, he had been on the field for nearly twenty-seven hours. Little wonder that he wasn't able to bowl quite as much as some people would have liked.

21 Jack White was nicknamed 'Farmer' because of his ruddy complexion and because he was, in fact, a farmer!

The last Test match in the series took place back at Melbourne.[22] It started on the 8th March, 1929 and carried on till the 16th March. For England, Herbert Sutcliffe and the captain, Percy Chapman, were injured. Maurice Leyland and Ernest Tyldesley who took their places were both very fine players and more evidence of England's strength in depth when it came to batting. Jack White took over the captaincy.

England won the toss and chose to bat. Jack Hobbs scored the last of his twelve centuries against Australia and Maurice Leyland chalked up his first. Jardine was the new opening partner for Hobbs and he gave evidence of his famous obduracy by scoring 19 off 126 balls. Hammond 'failed', only scoring 38 and England were all out for 519.

Woodfull and Bradman both got centuries as Australia accumulated 491 at less than two runs an over. Two scores of around 500 at a relatively slow rate would make a draw a near certainty these days but this was a fight to the finish. When England batted again, Jardine was out first ball and the tourists struggled to a total of 257. Hobbs top scored with 65 but once again Hammond missed out. Australia only needed 286 to win and were in with a chance to salvage some pride from the series.

Wally Hammond now showed what he could do with the ball when he wasn't too tired from scoring centuries and took 3 for 53 off twenty-six overs. However, Jack Ryder, the Australian captain, and Don Bradman saw their side home with 5 wickets to spare. The 'whitewash' had been avoided.

Hammond had scored 905 runs, by some way a record for a Test series. He was not to know that it would be beaten so soon, by Bradman when the Australians visited England the following year. They remain the only two players to have scored over 900 runs in a series. A rivalry between the two cricketers continued

22 The WACA at Perth did not become Australia's fifth Test venue until 1970.

up to the outbreak of the Second World War and resumed after it. Hammond had undoubtedly had the better of the 1928/29 tour but Bradman took the honours when the Australians toured in 1930 and in every Ashes series in which they both competed thereafter.

The 1928/29 tour saw Jack Hobbs pass on the mantle of England's greatest batsman to Wally Hammond. Hobbs was universally loved, referred to as 'the Master' and in 1953 became the first professional cricketer to be knighted. Hammond, on the other hand, remained an enigma to most of his fellow players, was admired rather than loved and received no honours at all (even Paul Collingwood got an MBE just for turning up at the Oval in 2005.)

A few days after returning from Australia in April 1929, Hammond married Dorothy Lister. By all accounts she was homely and good natured but no oil painting. She was the daughter of a cricket loving, wealthy textile merchant from Yorkshire. In truth, Hammond did not know her very well; it was a case of fame meets brass. Mrs. Merton's question to Debbie McGee springs to mind: "What was it that first attracted you to the millionaire Paul Daniels?"

She certainly wasn't the sort of woman that Hammond was normally attracted to. They had very little in common and the life of a professional cricketer would put pressure on even the happiest marriage. It is only relatively recently that players fly back in the middle of a Test series to be at the birth of their child. Nowadays, it is common practice for wives and children to join players on tour for Christmas and so on. In Hammond's day, a tour to Australia meant over six months away from home.

It seems that Hammond 'played away' a lot until he met Sybil Ness-Harvey in South Africa when he was captain of England on the tour of South Africa in 1938. She was beautiful and they fell in love. During the Second World War, Hammond was stationed at Cairo for a number of years and he flew down to Durban whenever he could. Later he was posted to South Africa which made things even easier.

Wally Hammond had finally found the woman he wanted to be with. They resolved to be married after the war ended and he had arranged for his divorce to go through. First though, Hammond was posted back to England in 1944. He was stationed at Regent's Park and conveniently had an office at St. John's Wood. Some of the buildings and area around Lords had been requisitioned by the RAF and Squadron Leader Hammond trained cadets there.

He also had the chance to play some cricket. Many games were played at Lords in the summer of 1944. It was seen as a morale boost for the public. On Whit Monday, a crowd of 30,000 saw England play Australia (effectively The Royal Australian Air Force). The one-day matches laid on in 1944 were hugely popular with the players and public alike. It makes you wonder why it took cricket another twenty years to realise the potential of this form of the game.

The war in Europe of course was still not over but when it finally was, in May 1945, five 'Victory Tests' were arranged around the country between an England XI led by Hammond and an Australian XI made up of Australian servicemen. Then, at the end of August, there was a showpiece match at Lords between England and the Dominions.

It was a classic game, described by *Wisden* as "one of the finest matches ever produced." In the context of the end of six years of world war, it certainly was. Wally Hammond captained England and Learie Constantine captained the Dominions. Keith Miller, a pilot with the RAF and not yet a Test player for Australia, scored a spectacular 185. The gifted Martin Donnelly had joined the New Zealand Expeditionary force as a private, moved to the Armoured Division, fought through the Italian campaign and arrived in England in 1945 as a Major. He scored a brilliant 133 for the Dominions. Wally Hammond scored a century in both innings for England. Learie Constantine, a black man leading ten white men, was outstanding in the field. His run-out of Phillipson precipitating a narrow victory for the Dominions.

County cricket resumed in 1946 and Hammond was back captaining Gloucestershire. He was top of the national averages once again that season and a tour of Australia was planned for the following winter. Having converted from professional to amateur in 1938 and captained England just prior to the war, Hammond was the natural choice to be captain. There were however lots of reasons for him not to go.

He was still the best batsman in England, even at the age of forty-three, but his physical powers were on the wane. He had been invalided out of the RAF at the end of 1944 because of fibrositis. (Strangely, both Bradman and Hutton were also discharged from the services on medical grounds.) The fibrositis affected Hammond's back and could strike at any time. He often played in pain in the summer of 1946 although few knew about it.

Even more pressing than his physical problems was his love life. His divorce proceedings were going through and he had brought Sybil, his wife-to-be, over from South Africa. Going on tour to Australia meant leaving Sybil on her own in England for over six months. She moved in with his mother although the two did not get on well. Despite the misgivings he must have felt, Hammond agreed to go on the tour to Australia; indeed he was keen to have one more go at the old enemy and bring back the Ashes. It would be a fitting climax to his career.

The boat voyage to Australia was relaxed and the England captain put his domestic troubles behind him. He saw the trip almost as a goodwill mission after both countries had suffered so much from the ravages of war. Bradman, with memories of the 'Bodyline' tour and England's 903 for 7 at the Oval in 1938, was to see it rather differently. The tour started well and Hammond scored a double century against Western Australia. Then, before the First Test, he received a phone call from Sybil. She couldn't get on with his mother and was moving out. She knew very few people in England and must have conveyed how miserable she was in a strange, cold, wet and ration-ravaged country.

Hammond, a difficult person at the best of times, immediately became withdrawn and hardly spoke to his team mates from then on. Much to the chagrin of his colleagues, he and the tour manager, Rupert Howard, used to travel by car between destinations. The rest of the team went by train. You don't have to have been on a management team building course to spot that this arrangement may not have been very conducive to team morale.

Details of Hammond's divorce were discussed by the press in England and then regurgitated in the newspapers in Australia. His back was giving him a lot of trouble. He had the mental turmoil of wondering whether 'the love of his life' would decide to abandon England and go back to the warmth and comfort of South Africa. Hammond was a man under extreme pressure. Not surprisingly, it affected his cricket.

Brian Sellars of Yorkshire CCC fame, a wonderful human being who once reprimanded Brian Close for calling Billy Griffith 'Billy' instead of 'Mr Griffith', did his bit to help. He was an England selector but was in Australia reporting for the *Yorkshire Evening Post*. Seemingly he saw no conflict of interest in these two roles and his press reports contained a continual stream of adverse comments about Hammond. Sellars probably would have said it was intended as constructive criticism but it is doubtful that Hammond saw it that way.

There was to be no repeat of the heroics of the 1928/29 tour. In the first four Tests, Hammond scored a total of 168 runs at an average of 21. Debilitated by his fibrositis, he was unable to play in the last Test. Australia's captain had rather better luck. Having scratched around for 28 in his first innings, Bradman survived a catch by Jack Ikin off Bill Voce. All the England team and most of the crowd thought he was out. Bradman, as was his right, didn't walk and the umpire gave him not out. He went on to score 187, and a lot more runs in the remaining Tests.

England lost the series 3 − 0. The weather, the umpiring and the fact that the team were just not good enough, all conspired to make Hammond's last visit to Australia a disappointing one. He did not protest or complain. He may have been taciturn and moody to the point of being morose but he was a genuine sportsman. The Australian public were warm in their treatment of him in the end. They recognized the dignified way that Hammond handled a difficult situation. Clif Cary, an Australian journalist, wrote: "Hammond did not think of himself. He displayed tact and diplomacy in the interests of cricket and wherever they went his colleagues were welcomed and liked."

There was one Test match in New Zealand on the way home. Hammond's back had recovered sufficiently to enable him to play and he scored 79 in a rain affected match. Apart from turning out for the MCC against Ireland in 1950, when he scored 92 not out, and an ill advised final appearance for Gloucestershire against Somerset in August 1951, that was it for Hammond as far as the first-class game was concerned. He married Sybil the day after arriving back from New Zealand. They moved into a house in Gloucestershire and by all accounts this was the happiest few years of Hammond's life. They later emigrated to South Africa and settled in Durban.

Walter Hammond was indisputably one of the greats of the game. His outstanding performance during the 1928/29 tour had set a marker that only Bradman has been able to better. He lost a whole year of cricket thanks to Lord Harris, another year to illness and, like so many other players, six years to the war. He still managed to score over 50,000 first-class runs at an average of 56.

The final tour to Australia in 1946 was a tour too many for Hammond. Had he not gone, he would have joined Bradman, Pollock, Headley and Sutcliffe in achieving the Holy Grail of a Test batting average of over 60. As it was he had to settle for 7,249 runs at an average of 58.45. In spite of all his idiosyncrasies, he was a modest man and he would have settled for that.

11. Ash Tree CC tour of Ibiza, 2010

In 2010, the Ash Tree Cricket Club decided to go for the Balearic hat trick. We had spread our largesse to Menorca and Mallorca; it seemed only fair to extend it to Ibiza as well. Luckily, one of our players knew the island well. In fact Mark, the one who raised the tea-making stakes by providing port and cheese, went there so often that it was almost his second home. He offered to organise the flights and hotel if there was enough interest for a tour within the club. His offer was accepted before he had finished the sentence.

Deposits were secured from a quorum of players and a game was fixed up for the 22nd May with the ICC (Ibiza Cricket Club, not the other lot). For some reason, whenever I told people I was going to Ibiza, they would start laughing. *The Rough Guide to Spain* describes Ibiza as "an island of excess........ famous for its clubbing scene." Cricket clubs were probably not what they had in mind but it would do for us.

Our Chairman, also called Mark, was due to celebrate his 65th birthday the day before the match. By his own admission, Mark is no great shakes as a cricketer. His batting ambition is to reach double figures – for the season. His bowling could probably best be described as "very slow filth", although he did get a hat trick a few seasons back when three batsmen in a row almost got a hernia trying to hit him into the next county and all missed.

Mark was one of the founding members of the Ash Tree CC when it began nearly forty years ago. He has been the guiding spirit of the club through good times and bad. Without him it is unlikely that the Ash Tree would have survived. So, it was really him that was responsible for us all being up at 4 o'clock in the morning heading for Manchester Airport.

In a bold but unsuccessful attempt to bring the average age of the touring party down below fifty, Mark had invited his son and son-in-law along to Ibiza. Both James and David had played for the Ash Tree in the past but had moved away some years ago and found better things to do with their lives. On reflection, it's difficult to think of many better things to do than play cricket for the Ash Tree but some people feel the need to move on with their lives I suppose. Although neither played regular cricket these days, or indeed any cricket, they had played in the past and, most importantly, were young, compared with the rest of the team anyway.

The early flight from Manchester left on time and somehow it didn't feel strange ordering a gin and tonic with breakfast at 7.30 in the morning. This may not have been quite in the David Boon[23] league of drinking but it started the tour off nicely.

Glorious sunshine greeted us when we arrived in Ibiza. The two mini-buses were ready and waiting and soon we were heading for our hotel in Santa Eulalia on the east coast of Ibiza. If you are looking for an acid house, techno trance, clubbing marathon

---

23 David Boon is renowned for setting the record, in 1989, for the number of 'tinnies' drunk on a flight between Sydney and London. He allegedly knocked back fifty-two, beating the record of forty-six set earlier by Rod Marsh. Apparently Marsh disputes the Boon record as he claims it included a stopover in Singapore, whereas all his 'tinnies' were drunk at 35,000 feet. Nevertheless, Boon seemingly managed to walk off the plane unaided and then attended a sponsor's cocktail party where he consumed another three pints. He then slept for thirty-six hours and missed two training sessions. Bobby Simpson, the Aussie manager, was not amused and fined him $5,000. Boon went on to score 442 runs in the Test series at an average of 55. All together quite an impressive performance!

experience then Santa Eulalia is probably not the place for you. It does, however, have plenty of cafés, bars, and restaurants, which was just fine by us.

The *Tropic Garden Hotel* was only a five-minute walk from the town and we soon headed off for our first beer of the day followed by lunch at a restaurant overlooking the port. Lunch seemed to merge seamlessly into dinner with only a stroll down the mile-long sea front promenade in between.

We were not only acclimatising and checking out the local sights, we were also on a recruitment drive for an extra player. Unfortunately for him and us, Bill, one of our best batsmen, had to cry off at the last minute. Our touring party therefore consisted of ten players and two ex-players. Of the last two, Calvin might have been tempted if all the bowling was going to be buffet style[24] but that was highly unlikely. Martin, the other 'non-playing' tourist, could rival Barry Sheene for the number of operations on his legs but said he would play if we couldn't find anyone else.

Mark, the organiser, was confident that we would find a likely candidate in one of the local bars but by the end of the evening we were lucky still to have ten players standing, let alone find an extra one. It would be bad form to turn up a player short. The Ash Tree prides itself on three things: playing the game in the right spirit, always putting out eleven players and the quality of its teas. We had one more recruitment opportunity the next day.

We had planned a special lunch to celebrate the birthday of Chairman Mark but before that, we were going to have some cricket practice. This took the form of a game of beach cricket in full public view. Potentially embarrassing but it might attract some likely candidates for the team. One guy – youngish and a cricketer – watched for a while and was keen to play. His wife seemed less

---

24 Help yourself.

enthusiastic but marital strife was averted when it was established that they were flying home the next day and the timing meant that they might miss their plane if he played.

We continued with our intensive practice on the beach. The bounce was low and slow. The bowling was reduced to gentle lobs that were either dispatched with great force or missed completely. With a trademark pull to leg, Chris smashed his first ball in the direction of the beach bar where Martin and Calvin were sitting watching the game and supping their beers. Martin nonchalantly put out his right hand and caught the ball without spilling a drop from the glass held in his other hand. We had found our eleventh player. As long as Martin could take his chair and beer along, he'd be fine.

Our power hitting had burst the special 'cricket tennis ball' which had come all the way from Australia. Three local replacement balls purchased at the beach lasted even less time and so there was nothing left to do but go in search of our lunchtime destination. This was *Yemanja*, a beach-side restaurant at Cala Jondal in the south of Ibiza. We later learned that this location was very much on the A-list and, in retrospect, we were a little disappointed not to be recognised and feted as celebrities.

Nevertheless, we had a good table with fabulous views. With no disrespect intended to the ladies of Macclesfield and Bollington, there were sights there that you would not normally see on a walk down Macclesfield High Street. You would have to wear a bit more for a start otherwise you could get a nasty chill.

The food and wine were splendid and the ambience excellent. It was a fine way to celebrate a birthday or indeed anything else. Crawford shared a story with us that he had just read on his iPhone. A man had been apprehended shagging a sheep behind the library in Bollington. Some of the team who lived in Bollington were shocked. They hadn't realised there was a library in Bollington.

It seems that the world is increasingly divided into those people who have iPhones and those who do not. If you own an iPhone then it seems to take over your life. Rather like the characters in Philip Pullman's *His Dark Materials* trilogy, who can not survive for long if they are separated from their animal shaped dæmons, anyone who is parted from their iPhone is distraught. Pulman describes these characters as being faceless and with their hearts torn out – unnatural creatures, not of this world.

If you happen to see someone like this wandering around, it probably means that they have lost their iPhone. It has to be said that iPhones, if used in moderation, can be useful. For instance, checking outrageous claims made by Tony, one of our players on tour. One example was when he claimed that a city in China produces 90% of the world's socks.[25]

iPhones are also great for checking song titles or film titles that are on the tip of you tongue but just can't remember. They must be very helpful in pub quizzes if you can get away with it.

The day of the match dawned and amazingly all players were present and correct at the appointed time. Our offer to play a second game on Sunday had been declined and so this was to be our only game. As we clambered aboard the minibuses, there was a sense of anticipation among the tourists that could almost be interpreted as enthusiasm. Mad dogs and Englishmen go out

---

25 Actually, this is nearly true. The town of Datang, just south of Shanghai, is known as Sock City. It produces an astonishing fourteen billion pairs of socks each year - around two sets for every person on the planet. In the late 1970s, Datang was little more than a rice-farming village with 1,000 people who gathered in small groups and stitched socks together at home, and then sold them in baskets along the highway. Government officials branded Datang's sock makers as 'capitalists' and ordered them to stop selling socks. Now they produce half the world's output, and the present government has nothing but praise for them.

in the midday sun, as the Noel Coward song goes, and we were indeed due to start the match at midday.

Ibiza CC play their cricket on a football pitch and we were keen to check out the Astroturf for pace and bounce and to make sure we had the appropriate footwear. Our attempt to gain a psychological edge by presenting a professional and organised image was somewhat undermined, as we stumbled out of the minibuses into the sunshine, by carrying our cricket kit in two suitcases and a number of carrier bags. As it happened, we had arrived so early that none of the opposition were at the ground. Consequently, we were able to play our first tentative practice shots on the Astroturf with no witnesses.

The opposition captain, called Jeremy, was the first to arrive. He seemed a decent bloke despite admitting to being both an estate agent and a Chelsea supporter, usually a combination to be wary of. Crucially, from an age point of view, he was our sort of vintage and so was his brother who arrived soon afterwards. However, as the rest of the team turned up, it was apparent that the two brothers were the only ones that fitted the normal Ash Tree age profile. The rest of the Ibizan team were twenty somethings and thirty somethings, and looked disconcertingly fit. The smattering of South African and Kiwi accents was also strangely unnerving.

Chris, our captain, began negotiations with Jeremy on the rules of engagement. The Ash Tree normally play 30 overs each innings, everyone bowls three overs, no LBW, batsmen retire when they get to 30 and come back at the end if everyone is out. However, we were the visitors so we would have to abide by what our hosts wanted. Jeremy agreed to the 30 overs – a football match was due to start at 5 o'clock anyway. He wasn't keen on everyone bowling three overs and eventually we agreed on a maximum of six overs per bowler. Neither was he happy about retiring at 30 so we had to let that one go. He did agree to the no LBW rule but probably regretted it later.

Looking at the opposition, we all felt that to bat first would be too risky as none of us wanted an embarrassingly early finish. By the time the fourth person had gone up to Jeremy and said that it might be a good idea if they batted first, I think he had got the message. They won the toss and batted.

I opened the bowling one end and David, one of our 'young' hopefuls, opened at the other. Very early in proceedings, David strained a hamstring. He managed to complete the over but, although he stayed on the field, he couldn't carry on bowling. Jeremy, who was umpiring at the time, came over to Chris and said that as David could not complete his bowling stint then our other strike bowler could bowl ten overs if we wished.

Chris looked confused for several minutes before he realised that Jeremy was referring to me. I bowl a sort of military medium in the sense that John Le Mesurier was part of the military in *Dad's Army*. I had bowled a tidy first over and then had a perfectly decent ball hit over extra cover for six. Chris thanked him for what at the time seemed like a generous gesture but in fact turned out to be a cunning plan.

Fears of a score well in excess of 200 proved to be unfounded. We took wickets at crucial times to slow the run rate and the fielding was surprisingly good throughout, with five excellent catches. Probably the pick of the catches was James' diving effort at deep square leg. This involved a combination dive incorporating a forward roll with half pike before eventually taking the ball in the prone position, all perfectly executed without disturbing his Panama hat or sunglasses.[26] As it was off me, obviously bowling to my field, I was particularly impressed.

---

26 I am indebted to Crawford Scholes for the description of this catch, which appeared in his Ash Tree match report. I did not feel I could improve on it.

Chris, the heat clearly affecting his judgement, had decided to take Jeremy up on his offer and had brought me back for a second spell, so I ended up bowling ten increasingly tired-looking overs. It didn't seem to be important at the time but would prove to be significant.

We held Ibiza to 183 for 6 off their 30 overs which was a lot better than we had feared earlier in the innings. If we could get off to a good start, a win was achievable. After much needed refreshments at tea, Mark, the organiser, and David, despite his hamstring, opened the batting. Mark is a big hitter and demonstrated this by hitting his second ball for six. If he could stay in for a few overs, we would be well on our way. Alas, it was not to be. He rather unluckily played on next over trying to hit another six. Hopes now rested with David who in his younger days had been a decent bat. Unfortunately, it wasn't to be his day and after hitting a good-looking boundary, he was bowled. 14 for 2 in the fourth over was not exactly the start we had hoped for.

Chris and Nick now came together and steadied the ship. They saw off the impressive opening bowlers and began to put runs on the board. There was plenty of chat from the fielders along the lines of "great dot ball Jim" and "good areas Robin" but the comments lacked the sense of irony that tends to accompany them in most normal Ash Tree games. 26 runs came off a new bowler in the 14th over, including a huge six over mid-on from Nick, and one could sense that Ibiza were getting a little concerned.

Chris began to carve[27] the bowling all over the park. Playing on a football ground with the cricket pitch marked out length ways from goal to goal, meant that the square boundaries were relatively short. I think it's fair to say that Chris favours the leg-side. With LBW out of the equation, it was an ideal situation for him.

27 Chris is a butcher by trade, arguably the best in Bollington.

Boundaries flowed from his bat, mostly through square leg and mid-wicket. Occasionally he would miss and the ball would strike his pads. Anguished appeals continually went up from bowler and fielders despite the no LBW rule.

Hitting yet another six over mid-wicket, Chris reached his 50, a rare occurrence for the Ash Tree given the usual 'retire at 30' rule. When Nick was eventually out, caught at deep mid-on, 96 runs had been put on for the third wicket, easily an all time Ash Tree record partnership for any wicket. Crawford joined Chris and the runs continued to come. 50 were needed off eight overs and a famous victory was in sight.

It was now that Jeremy played his trump card. He approached Chris and said that as our 'strike bowler' had bowled ten overs, it was only fair that some of their bowlers were allowed more than six overs. Chris had little option but to concede. Back came the opening bowlers, including the former Somerset colt bowler who had been difficult to get away in his first spell.

Crawford was out, trying to force the pace, and James took his place. He was soon out in a similar fashion. Wickets were falling but more importantly, the run rate had slowed. 25 runs were needed off two overs and Chris was facing the ex-Somerset colt. Despite seeing the ball like the proverbial melon, Chris played and missed at several deliveries before being bowled trying to hit the ball somewhere in the direction of Mallorca. He had scored 95, an Ash Tree record that is likely to stand forever.

Tony, from Somerset himself and who probably went to school with the bowler's grandfather, came out to face. Still 25 needed off one and a bit overs so victory was in the bag for Ibiza. Surely, a gentle one to let Tony get off the mark? No, a fierce beamer that Tony fended off with his glove. Two days later he was still going up to complete strangers in the street and showing them the bruise!

Our innings eventually finished at 162 for 6, 21 runs short of the target. Defeat with honour.

Chris had hit nine sixes and seven fours. He had missed his century by 5 runs but he was genuinely much more disappointed that we had lost. The Ibizan team went into a huddle at the end of the game, pleasure mixed with relief. We had a few beers after the match and then it was back to Santa Eulalia in the mini-buses.

That evening, half the touring party opted for tapas and the Champions League Final and the other half for tapas and not the Champions League Final. The Special One duly did the business for Inter Milan and then immediately moved onto his next challenge at Real Madrid. If Mourinho really wants to test himself, why doesn't he try managing England? Inter Milan were so impressed with the job that Rafael Benitez had done at Liverpool that, a week after he 'left by mutual consent', they offered him £2.5 million a year to be their new manager. Benitez's disappointment at leaving Liverpool was eased by being given a £4 million severance pay off. He lasted six months at Inter Milan before being sacked and getting another £2.5 million in compensation. Football is a funny old game isn't it?

Our evening ended, perhaps appropriately, in a bar called the Mirage where a band was just starting their encore of *Wild Thing*. Paul was tempted to enter the dance floor but resisted. Tony ("I can resist everything except temptation") was tempted and succumbed immediately. Again, I can do no better than to quote Crawford's tour report: "Tony prowled the dance floor with a glint in his eye that was part child in a sweet shop and part lion stalking a herd of wildebeest."

Sunday was the day after the night before and we had a gentle stroll along the sea front, reflecting on what might have been in the match against Ibiza and what never was going to be in the Mirage bar. It was soon time for lunch. Mark, using his local knowledge, booked us into The Gallery restaurant in Santa Eulalia. The food was brilliant and great value at 15 euro for a three-course meal. Sea bass and Yorkshire pudding made a surprisingly tasty combination for those that tried it.

The touring party, at this point feeling rather glad that Ibiza CC had not taken us up on our offer of a second game, moved on to a bar overlooking the harbour. Some sport was necessary even if cricket was not on the agenda so I suggested a friendly game of Spoof. For those that don't know the game, the rules are pretty simple.

Basically it is a guessing game involving coins. Each player takes a number of coins, between zero and three, from their pocket and holds them concealed within a clenched fist. The denomination of the coin is irrelevant, it's just the number that counts. The idea is then to guess the combined total number contained in all the players' hands.

One person starts by making a guess and then the play proceeds clockwise until everyone playing has guessed a number that hasn't previously been taken. This is a single round of the game. All players then reveal their coins and someone is 'out' if they chose the exact number. If this happens, the 'winner' (or non-loser) will then sit out the remaining rounds of this particular game and the others will play more rounds in the same way until only two players are left. This is 'the final', or crunch time, that decides the outcome of the contest.

Spoof can be a 'sociable' game to pass the time. Or it can be used to decide who buys the next round. Or, if you have someone like Mark, the organiser, in your party, it can escalate into something potentially unpleasant.

He decided that the 'winner', i.e. the last person left, would have to drink a forfeit. For reasons best known to himself, he went to the bar and asked for Baileys with a dash of cider. Baileys is a pretty dire drink on its own but when you add cider to it under the heat of the Ibizan sun, it becomes a rather unpalatable proposition.

Given his pulled hamstring and single figure score when batting, it was more or less preordained that David would complete a memorable twenty-four hours by having to drink the Baileys concoction. And so it proved.

Two more rounds followed, both 'won' by Crawford. The first forfeit was tequila and Tabasco with a peach schnapps chaser. The second was whisky and a raw egg. To the amusement of the other customers and the barely concealed admiration of the waitresses, he took them like a man (or words to that effect), probably glad of the three Yorkshire puddings he had consumed at lunchtime.

Crawford was keen to continue but the rest of us had seen enough. Relieved that we had escaped so far and worried what concoction Mark might come up with next, we made our excuses and left.

After freshening up at the hotel, it was time for our last night in Ibiza, volcanic ash permitting. Ending up in the bar that we had started in at the beginning of the tour (nice bit of symmetry for those who like that sort of thing), I found myself embroiled in one of those discussions that only happen in bars, late in the evening. The other participants, unfortunately for them, were Crawford and Nick.

The topic for discussion was who are your favourite Top Five musical artists? Or put another way, if you could only take the music of five performing artists to your desert island, who would they be? Now clearly, in this sort of debate, there can be no right or wrong answer. It is purely a question of personal choice. This did not prevent me from erupting at Nick's first selection of . . . . Queen.

"Queen! You can't be serious? They're so ephemeral."

Nick, somewhat taken aback by the vehemence of my response then suggested U2 as his second choice. Before I could launch into a tirade about U2 being the most overrated band in the universe and Bono being inordinately pleased with himself with very little justification, Crawford intervened to come up with his own somewhat 'left of field' choices. Alabama 3 was closely followed by the Proclaimers.

At this point Mark, the Chairman, joined us. When told of the subject of our discussion and asked for his musical choices, he thought for a moment and then started with .... Queen.

"Queen? But they're so ephemeral!" I spluttered.

Paul joined us and, sure enough, Queen featured in his Top Five. By this time, I had said 'ephemeral' so many times that I was no longer sure what it meant. I began to doubt my own sanity and had to go back to the hotel for a lie down.[28]

All the tour arrangements had gone so well that the next day, after an extended lunch at a pleasant beach-side restaurant, we headed for the airport in good spirits, confident that all would continue to go according to plan. The volcanic ash had stayed away, the flight out had been on time, the mini-buses were waiting as ordered and the hotel had been excellent. All the bases had been covered.

What we had not counted on was some climate change protesters cutting through the perimeter fence at Manchester Airport and chaining themselves to an aeroplane. The delay at Manchester had a knock on effect that meant we were stuck at Ibiza airport for several hours. After sitting in Ibiza's huge but

---

28 On being pressed for my own preferences, I came up with genuine rock royalty ... Dylan, Neil Young, Van Morrison, Bruce Springsteen, and I think Tom Waits got a mention.

soulless airport terminal for four hours, even the most liberal members of our touring party were all in favour of whichever plane the protesters had tied themselves to, just taking off and letting them have a closer look at the ozone layer. We eventually arrived home sometime after midnight.

After only a day's rest at home for me, it was down to Lords for the first Test against Bangladesh. I don't think everyone fully appreciates what a tough life being a cricket follower can be. Bangladesh won the toss and, possibly not wanting the game to be over too quickly, put England in. Maybe they were taking a leaf out of the Ash Tree's book by putting stronger opposition in to bat or, being more generous, maybe they were hoping to exploit the overhead conditions.

Alastair Cook certainly would have wished that they had been playing the Ash Tree 'no LBW rule' when he was adjudged leg before to a ball that Hawk-Eye subsequently showed was comfortably missing the stumps. This brought Jonathan Trott to the crease. It's difficult to get excited about Trott coming in to bat and I don't think it's just that he is South African. I was grateful that he had helped us win the Ashes with his century at the Oval in 2009 but he is somewhat uninspiring as a batsman. His pre-shot preparation is tedious and borderline obsessive compulsive behaviour. Quite why the umpires or match referee don't have a word with him about it is a mystery.

Strauss was supposed to be out of form but looked pretty good for his 83. Pietersen played a quirky innings and appeared to be still in Twenty:20 mode but without his usual number of runs in that form of the game. Bell flattered to deceive as he sometimes used to do, until he finally came of age on the 2010/11 Ashes tour. Notwithstanding the weight of Alastair Cook's runs, Ian Bell looked England's most fluent batsman in the series. Watching Trott bat, as we had to for the rest of the day, my immediate thoughts were that he tends to play the ball too far away from his body and that would be his downfall. Sure enough, that is how he was out, caught at backward point, but by then he had scored 226!

Except for perhaps Jonathan Trott's close relatives and the England bowlers, most of those watching at Lords on that first day, had been disappointed that Bangladesh had chosen to put England in as it had deprived us of the opportunity of seeing Tamim Iqbal bat. He is almost the antithesis of Trott as a batsman. Mercurial, entertaining, inventive, adventurous and a joy to watch.

Tamim scored 55 in the first innings and then hit a scintillating run-a-ball century in the second innings when Bangladesh followed on. He got through the 'nervous nineties' without too much trouble, moving from 87 to his century in four balls.

Despite Tamim's efforts, England won the match on the fifth day. It fell to Trott to hit the winning run and as the other players were leaving the field, he was still checking his mark at the crease. If his behaviour up to that point had been potentially OCD, this definitely crossed the line, so to speak. Very strange!

I tried my luck again with the first day of the second Test at Old Trafford, hoping to see Tamim in action. Unfortunately, England won the toss and chose to bat. When Strauss was out fairly early on, I thought I would have to sit through another day of watching Trott interminably making his mark at the crease. He only lasted five balls this time. Shafiul Islam, who hadn't played at Lords, bowled him between bat and pad. It is a terrible thing to say about someone batting for England but I was rather glad. In what must have been a pre-arranged tactic, Shafiul waited until Trott had gone through his laborious procedure and then, halfway through his run up, aborted it and started again. Trott was not able to go through his whole routine again and his concentration was broken. Trott's batting wasn't up to scratch this time and maybe he will have to rethink his approach, although it seemed to work OK when he helped England win the Ashes in Australia on the 2010/11 tour. Most of the rest of the day was taken up with a typically audacious innings from Pietersen and an elegant one from Bell.

When Bangladesh eventually batted on the second day, Tamim scored another run-a-ball century. A lucrative IPL contract next time around must be a formality and the first-class counties should be forming an orderly queue for his signature. Geoffrey Boycott and others don't think Bangladesh should be playing Test cricket but how else are they going to improve? No doubt people said the same thing when India were beaten 5 – 0 by England in 1959, but probably not Fred Trueman,[29] who took 24 wickets, or Brian Statham who topped both the batting and the bowling averages!

Bangladesh may have been given Test status a little too early, but when you see someone like Tamim Iqbal light up world cricket you know that the game is alive and well. Bangladesh tours will undoubtedly help the team to develop. A tour is an opportunity to play some cricket in unfamiliar surroundings. It is also a chance to meet new people and have new experiences. Not every player sees it that way. As Phil Tufnell put it so succinctly during England's tour of India in 1993: "I've done the elephant. I've done the poverty. I might as well go home."

I'm glad to say that the Ash Tree CC take a somewhat broader view. We have already planned our next tour. Having completed the Balearic hat trick we are starting all over again with another trip to Menorca. Our playing schedule is longer than usual: two games instead of the customary one. Following in England's

---

29 'Fiery Fred' had done even better in 1952 against India. He took 29 wickets in his debut series, including 8 for 31 in the first innings at Old Trafford when India were all out for 58.

successful footsteps, our pre-tour preparations will be exhaustive and, to ensure that we focus on the cricket, once again no WAGs will be coming on tour. We may not come back with the Ashes but we might well add the Sprinkler Dance to our repertoire.

Bibliography

Wisden Cricketers' Almanack   Many and various years
The cricketers' "bible".

Lords' Dreaming   Ashley Mallett
The full story of the 1868 Aboriginal Tour of England.

S.F. Barnes. His Life and Times   Andrew Searle
A biography of the great Staffordshire and England fast bowler.

Beyond a Boundary   C.L.R. James
Classic book about West Indian cricket and much more.

A Social History of English Cricket   Derek Birley
Examines the effect of English culture, class and history on cricket.

England versus Australia   David Frith
A pictorial history of over 100 years of Test matches.

The Penguin Cricketer's Companion   Edited by Alan Ross
An anthology of English cricket writing.

A Cavalcade of International Cricketers   Brian Crowley
An encyclopaedic review of over 1500 Test players.

Arlott on Cricket   Edited by David Rayvern Allen
A selection of John Arlott's writings on the game.

John Arlott's 100 Greatest Batsmen   John Arlott
Pen pictures of 100 great batsmen from Bobby Abel to Zaheer Abbas.

Nineteen Eighty-Four   George Orwell
    *The story of Winston Smith's battle with Big Brother, first published in
    1949.*

The Joy of Cricket   Edited by John Bright-Holmes
    A collection of essays and writings inspired by cricket.

Back Page Cricket   E.W. Swanton
    Cricket newspaper coverage from 1900 to 1987.

Invisible Republic   Greil Marcus
    The story of Bob Dylan's basement tapes.

Frank Worrell – A Biography   Ivo Tennant
    A biography of the outstanding cricketer and distinguished West Indian.

On Reflection   Richie Benaud
    An autobiography by the Australian Test all rounder and commentator.

Great Cricket Matches   Edited by Handasyde Buchanan
    Full length accounts of thirty famous cricket matches.

Gentlemen and Players   Michael Marshall
    With a Foreword by E.R. Dexter and Trueman, F.S.

Walter Hammond   Gerald Howat
    A biography of the great Gloucestershire and England cricketer.

Wally Hammond. The Reasons Why   David Foot
    Another biography of the great Gloucestershire and England cricketer.

The Wisden Papers 1888 – 1946   Edited by Benny Green
    *Benny Green selects the best essays written for Wisden Cricketers'
    Almanac.*

Starting with Grace   Bob Willis and Patrick Murphy
    A pictorial celebration of cricket from 1864 to 1986.

Also from Loose Chippings Books

The Cheesemonger's Tales
A good read for all food and wine lovers

Not Dark Yet
A very funny book about cricket

Cool Is The Reaping
Poems of rural England

Diary of a Shropshire Lass
A delightful autobiography

The Harts of Chipping Campden
Essential reading for all who admire the town or fine silver

Keeping Afloat
A light hearted tale of exploits on the canals of France

Roy The Eagle
Children's Picture Story Book about how what makes us different brings us together

Walk With The Wise
Reflections on thought-provoking quotations to stimulate and guide those who are interested by life's challenges

Call of the Litany Bird
Surviving the Zimbabwe Bush War

Full details from our website
www.loosechippings.org